SPECTRUM®
Critical Thinking for Math
Grade 4

Published by Spectrum®
an imprint of Carson-Dellosa Publishing
Greensboro, NC

Spectrum®
An imprint of Carson-Dellosa Publishing LLC
P.O. Box 35665
Greensboro, NC 27425 USA

ISBN 978-1-4838-3551-8

03-192177811

Table of Contents Grade 4

NAME _____

Check What You Know

Adding and Subtracting Through 5-Digit Numbers

Draw a model to find the missing number.

1. __213__ + 117 = 310

Draw a number line to find the missing number.

2. __5605__ + 15,978 = 30,583

3. Audrey works at a garden shop. This year, she sold 2,429 seed packs, 1,339 indoor plants, and 2,117 outdoor plants. How many items did Audrey sell in all? Use the partition method to show your work.

Check What You Know

Adding and Subtracting Through 5-Digit Numbers

Draw a model to find the missing number.

4. _160_ – 364 = 524

Draw a number line to find the missing number.

5. 47,893 – 45704 = 2,096

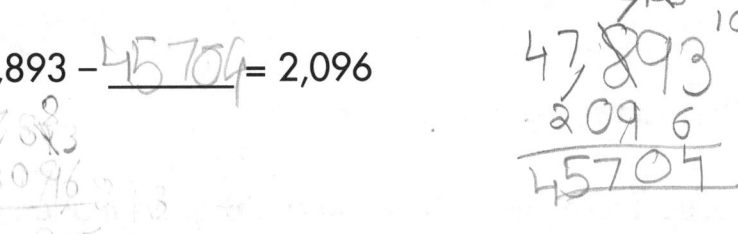

6. A baseball team gave away free hats to some of the fans that attended the game. There were 13,786 people at the game, and 2,959 fans did not get hats. How many fans did get hats?

7. At the same baseball game, the concession stand sold 1,245 hot dogs, 2,974 orders of nachos, and 3,945 ice cream sandwiches. How many total food items did the concession stand sell?

Lesson 1.1   Addition and Subtraction in the Real World

Jackie has 46 stamps in her collection, and Irene has 23 stamps. How many stamps do Jackie and Irene have altogether? Jackie will get 10 more stamps for her birthday. How many stamps will Jackie and Irene have after Jackie's birthday?

First, add what Jackie and Irene have now: $46 + 23 = 69$
Then, add the 10 stamps that Jackie will get for her birthday: $69 + 10 = 79$

Jackie and Irene will have 79 stamps altogether after Jackie's birthday.

Solve. Write the addition or subtraction sentences you used.

Yuri's soccer team is in the State Cup Tournament. There were 78 goals made in the entire tournament. Yuri's team made 29 of the goals. How many goals did the other teams make?

$$\begin{array}{r} 6\,\overset{7}{\cancel{8}}\,10 \\ 2\,9 \\ \hline 4\,9 \end{array}$$

The other team made 49 goals

Elena's team scored 16 goals in the tournament. How many goals did Yuri's team and Elena's team score altogether?

$$\begin{array}{r} 2\,9 \\ 1\,6 \\ \hline 4\,5 \end{array}$$

They scored 45 goals

Lesson 1.2   Finding Unknowns

To find an unknown addend in an addition problem, subtract the given numbers.

$52 + ? = 81$ ⟶ $\begin{array}{r} {}^{7}\ {}^{11} \\ 8\!\!\!/\,1\!\!\!/ \\ -\ 52 \\ \hline 29 \end{array}$ ⟶ $52 + \underline{29} = 81$

Find the unknown value. Write the subtraction problem you used.

$\underline{536} + 448 = 984$

$\begin{array}{r} 9\,{}^{7}8\,{}^{}4\!\!\!/\,{}^{10} \\ -\ 4\ 4\ 8 \\ \hline 5\ 3\ 6 \end{array}$

$536 + 448 = 984$

$4,251 + \underline{5,619} = 9,870$

$\begin{array}{r} 9,8\,{}^{6}\,{}^{}7\!\!\!/\,{}^{10} \\ -\ 4\,2\,5\,1 \\ \hline 5,6\,1\,9 \end{array}$

$4,251 + 5,619 = 9,870$

Adrian had 155 marbles. Her friend Beth also had some marbles. Together, Adrian and Beth had 481 marbles. How many marbles did Beth have? How many would they have if Adrian found 5 more marbles?

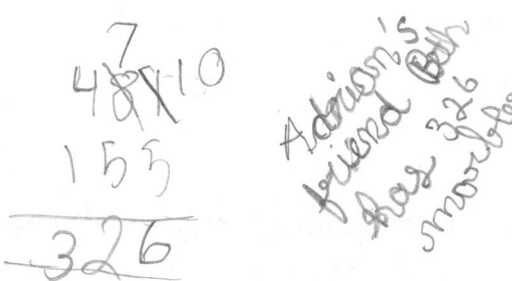

$\begin{array}{r} 481 \\ 5 \\ \hline 486 \end{array}$ They would have 486 marbles

$\begin{array}{r} 4\,{}^{7}8\,1\!\!\!/\,{}^{10} \\ 1\ 5\ 5 \\ \hline 3\ 2\ 6 \end{array}$ Adrian's friend Beth has 326 marbles

Lesson 1.2 Finding Unknowns

To find an unknown subtrahend
in a subtraction problem,
subtract the given numbers.

minuend → 175 $\overset{6\ 15}{\cancel{175}}$ $175 - \underline{137} = 38$
subtrahend → – ?   – 38
difference → 38   137

To find an unknown minuend
in a subtraction problem,
add the given numbers.

minuend → ?   115 $132 - \underline{17} = 115$
subtrahend → – 17   + 17
difference → 115   132

Solve to find the unknown value.

$6{,}255 - \underline{3{,}742} = 2{,}513$

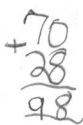

$$\begin{array}{r} {}^{5,000} \\ \cancel{6,255} \\ 2\ 513 \\ \hline 3742 \end{array}$$

$\underline{} - 329 = 171$

$$\begin{array}{r} {}^{+00} \\ 2\,829 \\ 171 \\ \hline 8 \end{array}$$

Bobbi saved some money from doing chores. He bought a computer game that cost
$28. Now, Bobbi has $70 left. How much money did Bobbi have to begin with?

$$\begin{array}{r} +70 \\ 28 \\ \hline 98 \end{array}$$

Does Bobbi have enough money left over to buy a new pair of sneakers that costs
$35 and a hat that costs $27?

$$\begin{array}{r} 35 \\ 27 \\ \hline 62 \end{array} \qquad \begin{array}{r} \cancel{98} \\ 62 \\ \hline 1 \end{array}$$

yes

Lesson 1.2 Finding Unknowns

You can use subtraction to find an unknown when adding three or more numbers.

1 + ? + 9 + 7 = 22

First, add the addends that are given: 1 + 9 + 7 = 17
Then, subtract: 22 − 17 = 5
1 + **5** + 9 + 7 = 22

Solve to find the unknown value. Write the addition and subtraction sentences you used.

<u>165</u> + 113 + 209 + 102 = 589

$113 + 209 + 102 = 424$

$$\begin{array}{r} 589 \\ -424 \\ \hline 165 \end{array}$$

Three friends had a picnic in the park. They each brought some fruit for dessert. One friend brought <u>6 bananas</u>, one friend brought <u>some pineapples</u>, and one friend brought <u>4 apples</u>. Altogether, the three friends had <u>12 pieces of fruit</u>. How many pineapples were there?

$$\begin{array}{r} 6 \\ 4 \\ \hline 10 \end{array} \qquad \begin{array}{r} 12 \\ 10 \\ \hline 2 \end{array}$$

If a fourth friend joins them and brings 5 peaches, how many pieces of fruit will there be altogether?

$$\begin{array}{r} 12 \\ 5 \\ \hline 17 \end{array}$$

If a fourth friend joins there will be 17 pieces of fruit

Lesson 1.3 Adding 3 or More Numbers

You can use a number line when adding three or more numbers.

$87 + 78 + \underline{\ \ ?\ \ } = 206$

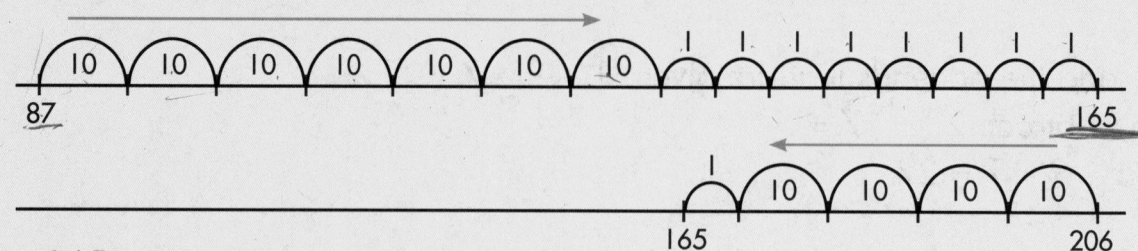

$206 - 165 = \underline{\ \ \ \ \ }$

$87 + 78 + \mathbf{41} = 206$

Use a number line to solve.

$315 + 173 + \underline{\ 200\ } + 166 = 854$

$315 + 173 + 166 = 654$

$\underline{\ \ \ \ \ \ \ } \ 200$

(handwritten right margin)
$\begin{array}{r} 315 \\ 173 \\ 166 \\ \hline 654 \end{array}$

Connor, Drew, and Jason are comparing their baseball card collections. Connor has 48 cards and Drew has 68 cards. Jason also has some cards. Together, the boys have 194 baseball cards. How many does Jason have?

   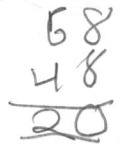   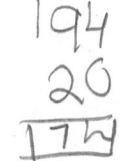

$\begin{array}{r} 68 \\ 48 \\ \hline 20 \end{array}$ $\begin{array}{r} 194 \\ 20 \\ \hline \boxed{174} \end{array}$

He has 174 cards

Jeremy joins them. He has 18 baseball cards in his collection. How many cards do the boys have with Jeremy's collection?

$\begin{array}{r} 194 \\ 18 \\ \hline 212 \end{array}$ 212

Lesson 1.4 Finding Unknowns

You can write a number sentence based on a completed number line.

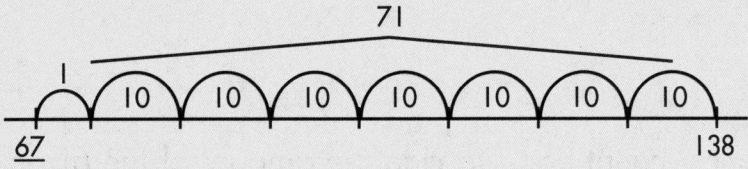

$$138 - 71 = 67 \qquad 67 + 71 = 138$$

Write the correct addition and subtraction sentence for each number line given.

$$\underline{651} - \underline{55} = \underline{596} \qquad\qquad \underline{596} + \underline{55} = \underline{651}$$

$$\underline{3475} - \underline{370} = \underline{3105} \qquad\qquad \underline{3105} + \underline{370} = \underline{3475}$$

$$\underline{57291} - \underline{1332} = \underline{55959} \qquad\qquad \underline{55959} + \underline{1332} = \underline{57291}$$

Lesson 1.4   Finding Unknowns

You can use a number line to find unknown addends in an addition problem.

$148 + ? = 464$

Using tens and ones, count backward to the amount of the given addend.

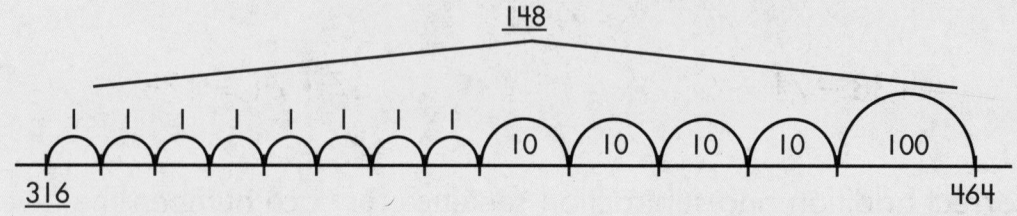

$148 + \textbf{316} = 464$

Subtract to find the missing addend. Use a number line to show your thinking.

____503____ $+ 247 = 750$

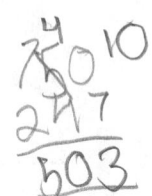

$\begin{array}{r} 7\,\overset{4}{5}0\,^{10} \\ 2\,7\,7 \\ \hline 5\,0\,3 \end{array}$

$3,482 +$ ____3107____ $= 6,589$

$\begin{array}{r} 6589 \\ 3482 \\ \hline 3107 \end{array}$

____3270____ $+ 18,805 = 51,510$

$\begin{array}{r} 51,510 \\ 18,805 \\ \hline 32700 \end{array}$

Lesson 1.4 Finding Unknowns

To find an unknown value in a subtraction problem, you can draw a picture.

7,198 − _____ = 5,806

Trade 1 thousand for 10 hundreds and subtract 800:

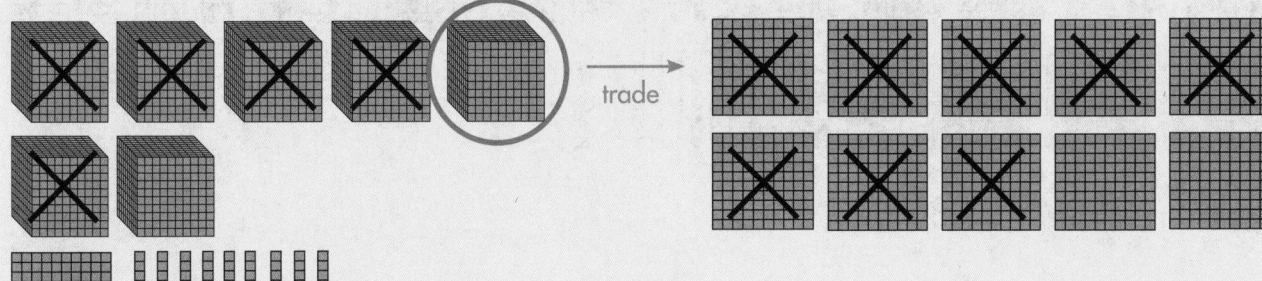

7,198 − 5,806 = 1,392 ; 7,198 − **1,392** = 5,806

Solve to find the unknown. Draw a picture to show your thinking.

3,700 − 2147 = 1,553

$$\begin{array}{r} 3,\overset{6}{\cancel{8}}\overset{90}{\cancel{0}}\overset{10}{0} \\ 1\ 5\ 5\ 3 \\ \hline 2\ 1\ 4\ 7 \end{array}$$

Lesson 1.4 Finding Unknowns

To find an unknown value when adding numbers, you can draw a picture.

4,909 + _____ = 6,989

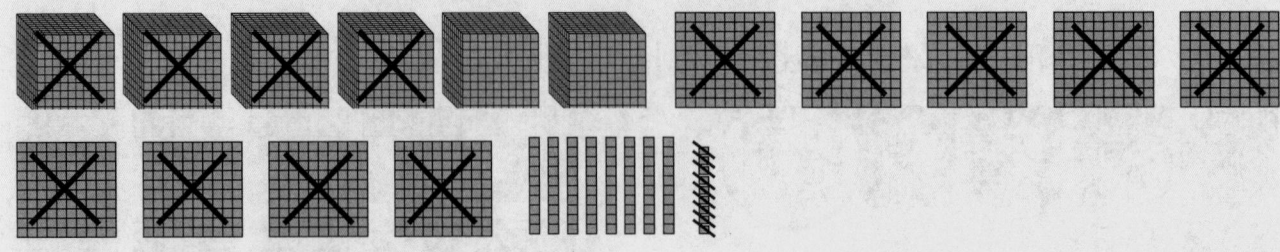

6,989 – 4,909 = 2,080

4,909 + **2,080** = 6,989

Solve. Draw a picture to show your thinking.

2448 + 10,336 = 12,784

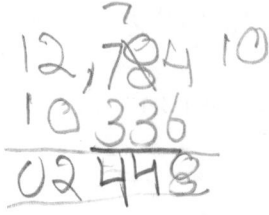

$$\begin{array}{r} 7 \\ 12,784 \ ^{10} \\ 10\ 336 \\ \hline 02\ 448 \end{array}$$

Lesson 1.4   Finding Unknowns

Solve the problems.

Draw a picture to show your work.
9,341 – ____3333____ = 6,007

$9,3\overset{3}{\cancel{4}}1\overset{10}{}$

$6,007$

3333

At the state fair, the candy booth had a swimming pool filled with chocolate-covered candies and fruit-flavored candies. A total of 88,547 candies were in the pool. At the end of the weekend, there were only 7,856 candies left. How many candies were given away at the state fair?

There were 80681 given away at the state fair.

$8\overset{7}{8},\overset{4}{5}\overset{100}{4}7$
$7,856$
80681

If 4,533 of the leftover candies were chocolate covered candies, how many were fruit-flavored candies?

$7\overset{1600}{8}0\overset{7}{6}8\overset{}{1}\overset{10}{}$
4533
76147

There are 76147 fruit-flavored

Lesson 1.4 Finding Unknowns

Solve the problems.

Draw a number line to show your work.

7,993 + <u>6814</u> = 14,807

Earth is 7,926 miles wide. Saturn is much wider. The total width of Earth and Saturn is 82,926 miles. How many miles wide is Saturn? Write the number sentence you used to solve.

82,926
7,426
75000

75000

If you add the width of Neptune, which is 15,125 miles, how many miles wide are all 3 planets?

Together the answer is 98051

82926
15125
98051

Lesson 1.5 Adding 3 or More Multi-Digit Numbers

You can use the partition method when adding three or more numbers.

2,012 + 150 + 150 = _____

thousands	2,000 + 0 + 0	= 2,000
hundreds	0 + 100 + 100	= 200
tens	10 + 50 + 50	= 110
ones	2 + 0 + 0	= 2

2,000 + 200 + 110 + 2 = 2,312

Solve. Use the partition method to show your work.

5,009 + 4,103 + 2,705 + 1,003 = _____

$5000 + 4000 + 2000 + 1000$

$5000 + 4000 + 2000 + 1000 = 12000$

$0 + 100 + 700 + 0 = 800$

$0 + 0 + 0 + 0 = 0$

$9 + 3 + 5 + 3 = 20$

12820

7,010 + 5,528 + 3,175 + 948 = _____

$7000 + 5000 + 300 + 0 = 150000$

$0 + 500 + 100 + 900 = 15000$

$10 + 20 + 70 + 40 = 140$

$0 + 8 + 5 + 8 = 21$

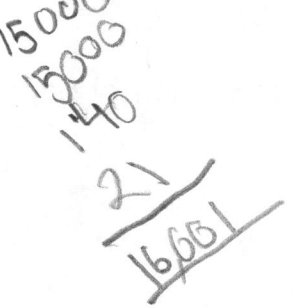

150000
15000
140
21
16651

Lesson 1.6 Addition and Subtraction in the Real World

Last year, 10,738 teenagers lived in Travis County. This year, 922 more teenagers moved there. How many teenagers live in Travis County now? Next month, 25 teenagers have birthdays and will no longer be teenagers. How many teenagers will live in Travis County after next month?

First, add how many teenagers lived in Travis County last year, and how many moved there this year: 10,738 + 922 = 11,660

Then, subtract the number of teenagers that have birthdays from the total number of teenagers in Travis County: 11,660 − 25 = 11,635

After next month, Travis County will have 11,635 teenagers.

Solve the problems. Show your work.

Over the weekend, the Dumon Theater sold 7,615 buckets of popcorn, 1,207 bottles of water, and 1,152 boxes of candy. How many food items did the theater sell?

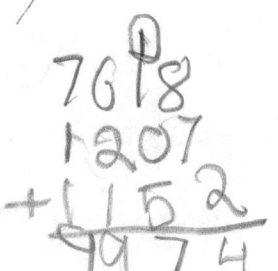

They sold 9974 of items

How many more buckets of popcorn than boxes of candy did the theater sell?

8867

Lesson 1.6 Addition and Subtraction in the Real World

Write a word problem to go with this addition problem. Then, solve.

$10,738 + 1,327 = 12065$

My friend had a lemomaid stand
she sealed 10,738 cups of lemomaid
I saild 1327 cups of lemomaid. How many
cups of lemomaid did we have together

Write a word problem to go with this addition problem. Then, solve using the partition method.

$1,935 + 1,690 + 130 + 117 = 3872$

pen is sloved The promlem
adove and ne got 382 is it
right if mot wright the right answer

Lesson 1.7 Checking Answers

You can check a subtraction problem by using addition.

$1,971 - 466 = 1,055$
$1,055 + 466 = 1,521$ This answer is not correct.

Solve the problem again and recheck.

$$\begin{array}{r} \overset{6\ \ 11}{1,9\cancel{7}\cancel{1}} \\ -\ \ 466 \\ \hline 1,505 \end{array} \qquad \begin{array}{r} \overset{1}{1,505} \\ +\ \ 466 \\ \hline 1,971 \end{array} \checkmark \text{ This answer } \textbf{is} \text{ correct.}$$

Use addition to check the problems. If the answer is incorrect, solve the problem again and recheck. Write the addition sentence you used to check.

$512 - 167 = 287$ $20,897 - 4,187 = 17,191$

wrong
not correct

$167 + 287 = 454$
$\begin{array}{r} 287 \\ 167 \\ \hline 454 \end{array}$

not correct

$17191 + 4187$

$\begin{array}{r} 17197 \\ 4187 \\ \hline 21384 \end{array}$

Lesson 1.7 Checking Answers

You can check an addition problem by using subtraction.

$14,011 + 25,126 = 40,137$
$40,137 - 25,126 = 15,011$ This answer is incorrect.

Solve the problem again and recheck.

$$\begin{array}{r} 14,011 \\ + 25,126 \\ \hline 39,137 \end{array} \qquad \begin{array}{r} 39,137 \\ - 25,126 \\ \hline 14,011 \end{array} \quad \checkmark \text{ This answer } \textbf{is} \text{ correct.}$$

Use subtraction to check the problems. If the answer is incorrect, solve the problem again and recheck. Write the addition sentence you used to check.

$43,106 + 19,847 = 75,103$ 　　　　　　　 $1,599 + 3,100 = 4,998$

Check What You Learned

Adding and Subtracting through 5 Digits

Read the problem carefully and solve. Show your work under each question.

Four Boy Scout troops collected canned goods to donate to the Rossville food bank. At the end of the week, Troop 151 had 92 cans. Troop 152 had 213 cans. Troop 153 had 88 cans and Troop 154 had 105 cans.

1. How many more cans did Troop 152 and 154 collect than Troop 151 and 153? Show your work using a number line.

2. The scouts in Troop 154 brought in more cans the following week, raising their total to 366 cans. How many cans did the students add in the following week? Draw a picture to show your work.

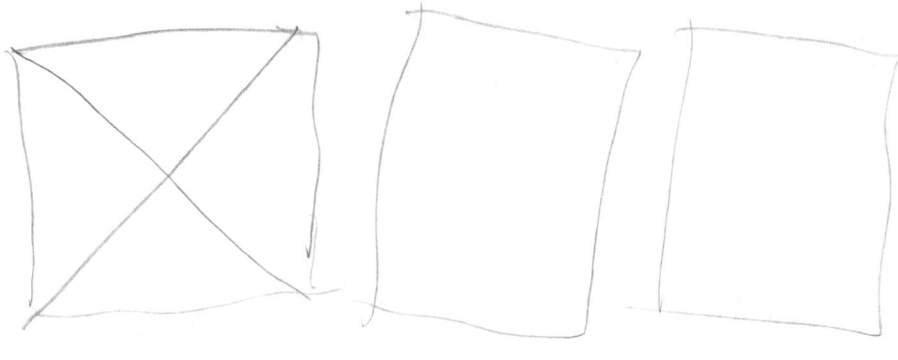

Check What You Learned

Adding and Subtracting through 5 Digits

Read the problem carefully and solve. Show your work under each question.

The Penny Club at Avery Elementary School collects pennies and donates them to a local charity every fall and spring. There are 4 members of the club: Kelly, Oliver, Pablo, and Reese. The following chart shows how many pennies each member collected last fall and spring.

Member	Fall	Spring
Kelly	5,899	16,522
Oliver	45,784	13,524
Pablo	9,632	85,211
Reese	963	48,599

3. How many more pennies did the club donate in the spring than in the fall? Use the traditional methods to show your work.

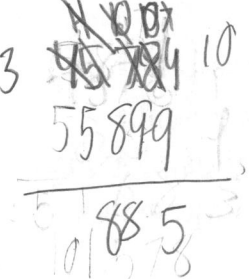

4. Which member donated the most pennies last year?

5. What is the total of the 3 highest amounts of pennies donated in the spring? Show your work using the partition method.

NAME _____

Check What You Know

Numeration

Andrew is thinking of a number. The number has a 3 in the tens place. The number in the ones place is three more than 5. There is a 6 in the ten thousands place. The number in the hundreds place is between 0 and 2. The number in the thousands place is 5 less than 10.

Fill in the blanks for Andrew's number.

1. Number name: _____

2. Expanded form: _____

3. Round the number to the nearest thousand: _____

Jonathan is thinking of a number. This number has a 9 in the thousands place as well as in the 2 places to the right. The number in the ones place is double the number in the ten thousands place. The number in the hundred thousands place is 6. The number in the ten thousands place is 4 less than 6. The number in the millions place is between 4 and 6.

Fill in the blanks for Jonathan's number.

4. Number Name: _____

5. Expanded Form: _____

6. Round the number to the nearest hundred thousand: _____

7. Compare Andrew and Jonathan's numbers using <, >, or =.

_____ ☐ _____

Lesson 2.1 Place Value

Numbers are made up of the digits 0–9 in different places. The place value of whole numbers goes from right to left. The chart below shows the place value of each digit in the number 1,359,264.

Place Value	1,000,000 Millions	100,000 Hundred Thousands	10,000 Ten Thousands	1,000 Thousands	100 Hundreds	10 Tens	1 Ones
	1	3	5	9	2	6	4
Digit Value	1,000,000	300,000	50,000	9,000	200	60	4

Answer the questions.

Isabella is thinking of a number in the hundred thousands. The first digit is equal to the number of digits in the number. The number has 20 tens and twice as many thousands. The number of ones is an odd number that is less than 5 and greater than the digit in the hundreds place. What is Isabella's number?

Using the digits 7, 8, 5, 9 and 2, write three numbers: the smallest number possible, the largest number possible, and a number between the largest and smallest numbers.

Lesson 2.2 Writing Numbers

There are 3 ways to write numbers:

Standard form Using numerals, place a comma every 3 digits going from right to left: 25,845

Number name Using words, include each digit as well as its place value: twenty five thousand eight hundred forty five

Expanded form Shows how each digit is multiplied by its place value: $(2 \times 10,000) + (5 \times 1,000) + (8 \times 100) + (4 \times 10) + (5 \times 1)$

Write the missing forms of each number.

standard form	78,985
number name	
expanded form	

standard form	
number name	two hundred seventy-six thousand four hundred thirty
expanded form	

standard form	
number name	
expanded form	$(4 \times 1,000) + (3 \times 100) + (4 \times 1)$

Lesson 2.3 Rounding

To round 56,348 to the nearest thousand, follow these steps.
1. Find the digit in the thousands place: 5<u>6</u>,348.
2. Look right. The digit in the hundreds place will decide if the digit in the thousands place gets rounded up to 7 or stays the same at 6.
3. The digit in the hundreds place is 3. Since 3 is less than 5, the digit in the thousands place, 6, stays the same.
4. All digits to the right of the thousands place become zeros.
5. 56,348 rounded to the nearest thousand is 56,000.

Round each number to all of the nearest place values.

187,349

tens: _____

hundreds: _____

thousands: _____

ten thousands: _____

hundred thousands: _____

58,045

tens: _____

hundreds: _____

thousands: _____

ten thousands: _____

hundred thousands: _____

567,503

tens: _____

hundreds: _____

thousands: _____

ten thousands: _____

hundred thousands: _____

285,393

tens: _____

hundreds: _____

thousands: _____

ten thousands: _____

hundred thousands: _____

Lesson 2.3 Rounding

Read each problem carefully. Round the numbers given to the nearest place value given.

Callista is writing a report about the recent election for the district attorney of her state. The chart below shows how many votes each candidate received.

Candidate	Votes
Mrs. Benson	2,431,584
Mr. Ling	547,965
Ms. Shaw	249,632

Callista wants to round the number of votes Mrs. Benson received. What is this number rounded to the nearest million?

What is the number of votes Ms. Shaw received rounded to the nearest ten thousand?

Callista rounds the number of votes Mr. Ling received to the nearest hundred thousand. What does she get for an answer?

To determine how many people voted in the election, Callista rounds each candidate's total votes to the nearest hundred thousand and added them together. What does she get for an answer?

Lesson 2.4 Comparing Numbers

To compare the numbers 12,317 and 12,713, line them up as shown below. This shows you which digits have the same place value.

ten thousands	thousands	hundreds	tens	ones
1	2	3	1	7
1	2	7	1	3

Begin with the digit farthest to the left. Both numbers have 1 in the ten thousands place and 2 in the thousands place. The digits in the hundreds place (3 and 7) are different, so use them to determine which number is greater.

The symbols > (greater than), < (less than), and = (equal to) are used to compare numbers.

$$12{,}713 > 12{,}317 \qquad OR \qquad 12{,}317 < 12{,}713$$

Order the set of numbers from **least** to **greatest**.

5,635,042   5,653,024   5,536,204   6,536,042

Four friends each had a coin collection. Darius had 45,673 coins in his collection. Forrest had 46,537 coins in his collection. Evan had 45,637 coins in his collection, and Jaime had 44,657 coins in his collection. Order the friends' coin collections from **greatest** to **least**.

Lesson 2.4 Comparing Numbers

Noah and Molly are playing a math game called Number Spin. They spin a spinner labeled 1 – 9 and use each number they spin to make larger numbers. They change the number of digits in the numbers they create each round. The chart below shows the numbers they made each round.

Round	Noah	Molly
1	5,965	5,874
2	2,631,891	2,555,873
3	94,321	84,110
4	544,331	975,211

Write <, >, or = to compare Noah and Molly's numbers from round one.

5,965 _____ 5,874

Molly wants to compare the numbers in round three. What should she write to compare them?

Who made the larger number in round four? Compare the 2 numbers using <, >, or =.

Check What You Learned

Numeration

Write the smallest and the largest number you can make with each set of digits.

7, 5, 2, 8, 4

   1. Largest: _____

   2. Smallest: _____

6, 3, 1, 7, 9

   3. Largest: _____

   4. Smallest: _____

Compare the two largest numbers and two smallest numbers above using **<**, **>**, or **=**.

   5. Largest Numbers

   _____ ☐ _____

   6. Smallest Numbers

   _____ ☐ _____

7. Write the largest of the four numbers in expanded form:

_____

8. Write the smallest of the four numbers as a number name:

_____

9. Round the largest number to the nearest ten thousand. _____

10. Round the smallest number to the nearest thousand. _____

Check What You Know

CHAPTER 3 PRETEST

Multiplication and Division

Read carefully and solve. Show your work under each question.

Tiffany places an order for office supplies. She orders 18 boxes of blue pens. There are 45 pens in each box. Paperclips come in boxes of 1,543, and she orders 6 boxes. She orders 12 boxes of rulers, and 105 come in each box.

1. How many total paperclips does Tiffany order? Show your work using the traditional method.

2. How many rulers does Tiffany order? Show your work using the grid method.

3. When Tiffany receives the order, she finds that 7 of the 18 boxes are filled with red pens instead of blue pens. How many blue pens does Tiffany have from this order?

Check What You Know

Multiplication and Division

Read carefully and solve. Show your work under each question.

Walsh's Hardware is having a big sale. The staff workers are gathering tools and other items into groups for the sale.

4. Benjamin's boss gives him 4,304 bolts. His boss says to put them in bags of 8 bolts each. How many full bags of bolts will he have? Will he have any left over? If so, how many? Show your work using the partial quotients method.

5. Brooke has 732 screwdrivers. She puts them in sets of 5. How many screwdrivers will be left over when she is finished? Show your work using long division.

6. The sale items are worth $8,958 in all. The sale will last for 3 days. How much money will the store make per day if the sales are equal each day? Show your work using short division.

Lesson 3.1   Prime and Composite Numbers

A number is called prime if its only factors are 1 and itself. For example, 7 is a prime number. The only factors of 7 are 1 and 7.

A number is called composite if it has more than two factors. For example, 8 is a composite number. 1, 2, 4, and 8 are all factors of 8.

A factor tree is a tool that breaks a number down into its prime factors.

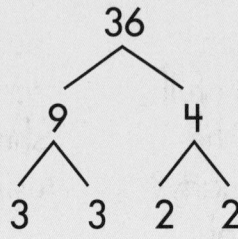

List the factors of each number. Then, label each number as prime or composite.

Number	Factors	Prime or Composite?
7		
18		
29		

Write 2 composite numbers and create factor trees for each.

_____   _____

Lesson 3.2 Multiplication: Traditional Method

$$\begin{array}{r} \overset{1}{72} \\ \times\ 8 \\ \hline 6 \end{array}$$

← Put 6 under the ones place.
Add the 10 above the 7.

Multiply 2 ones by 8.
$2 \times 8 = 16$ or $10 + 6$

$$\begin{array}{r} \overset{1}{72} \\ \times\ \ 8 \\ \hline \underline{5}\,\underline{7}\,6 \end{array}$$

Multiply 7 tens by 8.
Then, add 1 ten.

$70 \times 8 = 560 \rightarrow 560 + 10$
$= 570$ or $500 + 70$

Answer the questions. Show your work.

There are 38 chicken farms near a New York town. Each farm has 7 barns and in each barn are 78 chickens. How many chickens are on each farm?

How many total barns are there?

Lesson 3.2 Multiplication: Grid Method

704 × <u>8</u> = _____

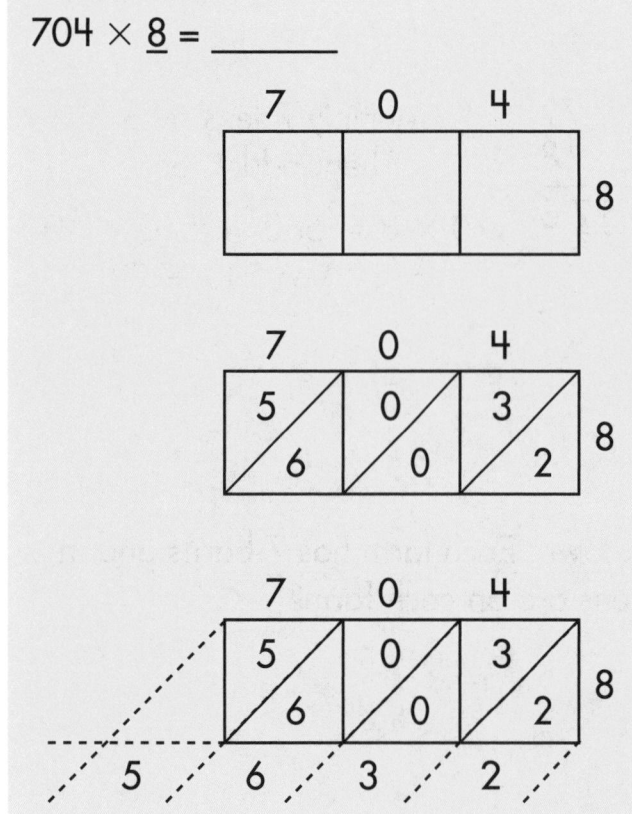

Make a 3–by–1 grid. Put the first number on top and the second number on the side.

Divide each square in half and multiply each pair of digits: 4 x 8, 0 x 8, and 7 x 8. For example, 4 x 8 = 32, so write 3 above the diagonal and 2 below it.

To find the answer, add along the diagonals. Regroup as needed.
704 x 8 = 5,632

Answer the questions and show your work.

In a tropical rain forest, the average annual rainfall is about 180 inches. After 9 years, about how much rain will have fallen in the rain forest? Use a grid to multiply.

During year 10, the amount of rain measured was 245 inches. How much total rain has fallen in the last 10 years?

Lesson 3.3 Multiplication: Repeated Addition

You can multiply using the repeated addition method.

3,421 x 3 = _____

$$
\begin{array}{r}
3,421 \\
3,421 \\
+\ 3,421 \\
\hline
10,263
\end{array}
$$

Answer the questions using repeated addition. Show your work.

A school of 1,786 students went on a field trip to collect sand dollars. If the students collected 4 sand dollars each, how many sand dollars did they collect?

A different school of 2,641 students also went on a field trip and collected seashells. If each student from that school collected 5 seashells each, how many total sand dollars and seashells did the schools collect?

Lesson 3.4 Multiplication Tables

To complete a multiplication table, multiply all the numbers in the **In** column by the same number to get the answer in the **Out** column.

Rule: Multiply by 3

In	Out
3	9
4	12
5	15

Complete each table.

Rule: Multiply by 19

In	Out
1	
3	
6	
9	

Rule: Multiply by 1,526

In	Out
2	
3	
4	
5	

Rule: Multiply by 7 and add 12.

In	Out
515	
894	
202	
485	

Lesson 3.5   Multiplication

Write a word problem to go with this multiplication problem. Solve using the traditional multiplication method.

$71 \times 67 =$

_____

_____

_____

_____

Solve this problem using the grid method. Show your work.

$841 \times 71 =$

Lesson 3.6 Multiplication in the Real World

A cable program loans channel boxes to 19 community centers for a trial program. If there are 13 boxes for each center, how many boxes are being loaned? Four more community centers would like to join the program. How many more channel boxes will be needed?

To answer the first question, multiply 19 community centers by 13 channel boxes. 247 boxes are being loaned.

$$
\begin{array}{r}
{\scriptstyle 2} \\
19 \\
\times\ 13 \\
\hline
57 \\
+\ 190 \\
\hline
247
\end{array}
$$
} add

To answer the second question, multiply 13 channel boxes by 4 community centers. 52 more boxes will be needed.

$$
\begin{array}{r}
{\scriptstyle 1} \\
13 \\
\times\ 4 \\
\hline
52
\end{array}
$$

Solve the problems. Show your work.

Orlando's Orchards grows 2 types of apples. One is red and the other is green. The trees that grow red apples are planted in 24 rows with 72 trees in each row. How many of the trees in the orchard grow red apples?

The trees that grow green apples are planted in 22 rows with 38 trees in each row. Next season, the orchard will add 3 more green apple trees to each row of green apple trees. How many total green apple trees will there be next season?

Lesson 3.7   Division Facts

9 ← quotient

divisor ⟶ 5 ⟌ 4 5 ← dividend

To check your answer, do the inverse operation.

If $45 \div 5 = 9$, then $5 \times 9 = 45$ must be true.

Using the division table, find 45 in the 5 column. The quotient is named at the beginning of the row.

5-column ⟶ **(divisors)**

(quotients)

quotient

x	0	1	2	3	4	5	6	7	8	9
0	0	0	0	0	0	0	0	0	0	0
1	0	1	2	3	4	5	6	7	8	9
2	0	2	4	6	8	10	12	14	16	18
3	0	3	6	9	12	15	18	21	24	27
4	0	4	8	12	16	20	24	28	32	36
5	0	5	10	15	20	25	30	35	40	45
6	0	6	12	18	24	30	36	42	48	54
7	0	7	14	21	28	35	42	49	56	63
8	0	8	16	24	32	40	48	56	64	72
9	0	9	18	27	36	45	54	63	72	81

Complete the table below.

X	10	11	12	13	14	15	16	17	18	19
	100	110	120	130	140	150	160	170	180	190
	110	121	132	143	154	165	176	187	198	209
	120	132	144	156	168	180	192	204	216	228
	130	143	156	169	182	195	208	221	234	247
	140	154	168	182	196	210	224	238	252	266
	150	165	180	195	210	225	240	255	270	285
	160	176	192	208	224	240	256	272	288	304
	170	187	204	221	238	255	272	289	306	323
	180	198	216	234	252	270	288	306	324	342
	190	209	228	247	266	285	304	323	342	361

Lesson 3.8　Division: Long Division Method

$$8 \times 4$$

$$\begin{array}{r} 4 \\ 8\overline{)33} \\ -32 \\ \hline 1 \end{array}$$

33 is between 32 and 40, so $33 \div 8$ is between 4 and 5. The ones digit is 4.

x	1	2	3	4	5
8	8	16	24	32	40

Since $33 - 32 = 1$ and 1 is less than 8, the remainder 1 is recorded like this.

$$\begin{array}{r} 4 \text{ r } 1 \\ 8\overline{)33} \\ -32 \\ \hline 1 \end{array}$$

Divide using long division. Show your work.

$$7\overline{)8,921}$$

$$3\overline{)843}$$

Lesson 3.9 Division in the Real World

Two basketball teams carpool to their game. There are 23 players on Amanda's team. Each car for Amanda's team can hold 4 players. There are 22 players on Ben's team. Each car for Ben's team can hold 5 players. Ben's team has 4 cars.

How many cars can Amanda's team fill? How many players will be left over?

How many cars will Amanda's team need to take all the players to the game? Explain your answer.

Does Ben's team have enough cars to take all their players to the game? If not, how many players still need a ride?

Lesson 3.10 Division: Partial Quotients Method

The partial quotients method uses estimation to solve division problems.

First, draw a line down the right side of
the problem.
Think of easy numbers to decide how many 7s
can go into 87. Ten is an easy number.

You have 17 left. Again, think of an easy number
to decide how many 7s can go into 17. Two 7s is 14.

You have 3 left. Three is less than 7, so you are
done dividing.
Now, add the numbers you estimated
on the right side.
Your answer is 12 with a remainder of 3.

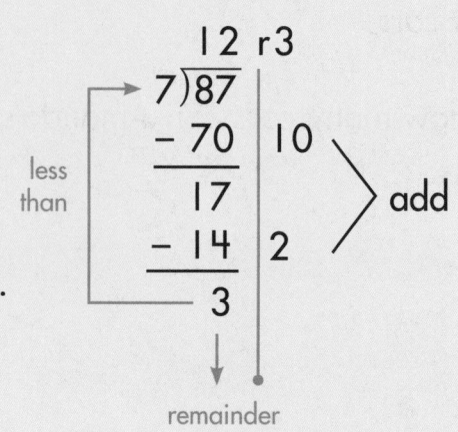

Divide using the partial quotients method. Show your work.

A service club went out to pick up litter in the park. They collected 558 bags of litter. If each member collected the same amount, how many bags did all 5 members collect? How many extra bags were collected?

Lesson 3.11 Division: Short Division Method

Short division is similar to long division, except that you complete the multiplication and subtraction in your head.

$$\begin{array}{r} 788 \text{ r2} \\ 5\overline{)3942} \\ \,_4\,_4 \end{array}$$

5 goes into 39 7 times. Write 7 on the line.
7 x 5 = 35. Mentally subtract: 39 – 35 = 4.

Write a small 4 between the 9 and the 4 to create 44. 5 goes into 44 8 times. Write 8 on the line.
5 x 8 = 40. Mentally subtract: 44 – 40 = 4.

Write a small 4 between the 4 and the 2 to create 42. 5 goes into 42 8 times. Write 8 on the line.

5 x 8 = 40. Mentally subtract: 42 – 40 = 2. This is the remainder. Your answer is 788 r2.

The school supply store received a shipment of 7,295 pens. If the pens are packed in 5 boxes, how many pens are in each box?

The store is supposed to receive 3 more boxes of pens tomorrow with the same number in each box. How many pens will the school supply store receive tomorrow?

Lesson 3.12 Division

Write a word problem to go with this division problem. Solve using short division.

$9\overline{)3466}$

_____

_____

_____

_____

Solve this problem using the partial quotients method. Show your work.

$7\overline{)4986}$

Lesson 3.13 Division in the Real World

Read the problem carefully and solve. Show your work under each question.

A textbook store is packing boxes full of books to ship. Each box can only hold one type of book. Each type of book must be divided evenly between each box. There are 148 mathematics textbooks and 78 literature textbooks. There are 40 music textbooks and 206 business textbooks.

If the literature textbooks are packed in 6 boxes, how many will be in each box?

The bookstore plans to use 9 boxes to ship the business textbooks. How many will fit in each box? How many will be left over?

If 5 music textbooks can fit into each box, how many boxes will the store need to ship all of them?

The store only has 4 boxes left to ship all of the mathematics textbooks. Will all the books fit or will there be some left over?

Lesson 3.14 Multiplication: Dividing to Find Unknowns

To find an unknown number in a multiplication problem, divide the two numbers you are given.

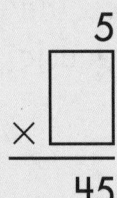

$$\begin{array}{r} 5 \\ \times \\ \hline 45 \end{array}$$

$$\begin{array}{r} 9 \\ 5\overline{)45} \\ -45 \\ \hline 0 \end{array}$$

$$\begin{array}{r} \square \\ \times 2 \\ \hline 1{,}870 \end{array}$$

$$\begin{array}{r} 935 \\ 2\overline{)1870} \\ -18\downarrow \\ \hline 07 \\ -6\downarrow \\ \hline 10 \\ -10 \\ \hline 0 \end{array}$$

Find each unknown number by dividing. Write the division problem you used.

$$\begin{array}{r} \square \\ \times 3 \\ \hline 8{,}454 \end{array}$$

$$\begin{array}{r} \square \\ \times 4 \\ \hline 144 \end{array}$$

Tyler had 3 boxes of matchbox cars in his toy room. His little sister dumped all of the boxes out onto the floor. There were 534 cars on the toy room floor. Tyler wants to put the cars back into the boxes. Each box held an equal amount of cars. How many toy cars were in each box?

 **Check What You Learned**

Multiplication and Division

Read carefully and solve. Show your work under each question.

Students at two schools are having a contest to collect soda cans and bottles for a charity drive.

1. Banksville has 643 students. Each student collects 31 cans during the contest. How many cans do the students collect altogether? Use the traditional method to multiply.

2. Oaktown has 189 students. Each student collects 9 bottles. How many bottles do they collect in total? Use the grid method to multiply.

3. The contest lasts 18 weeks. One student, Armando, collects 28 cans per week. How many cans does Armando collect during the contest? Use the traditional method to multiply.

Check What You Learned

Multiplication and Division

Solve each problem. Show your work under each question.

4. A diner has 195 seats, with 5 seats at each table. How many tables does the diner have? Use the partial quotients method to divide.

5. Dion buys 4 comic books every week. If Dion has 208 comic books, how many weeks has he been buying them? Use long division to divide.

6. The Underwood family drove 2,005 miles in 9 days. How many miles did the Underwoods drive each day if each day's mileage was the same? How many more miles did they drive on the last day? Use short division to divide.

Mid-Test Chapters 1–3

Read carefully and solve. Show your work under each question.

A local school is selling tickets for its basketball games. The chart below shows the number of tickets sold for the first 4 home games.

Game	Number of Tickets Sold
1	978
2	8,652
3	13,478
4	4,799

1. How many total tickets were sold for the first 4 home games? Use the partition method to add.

2. Write the answer in expanded form and number name form.

_____

_____

3. Out of the total number of tickets sold, only 11,956 people actually attended the games. How many people bought tickets but did not go to the games? Solve using a number line.

4. Round the answer to the nearest ten thousand: _____

Mid-Test Chapters 1–3

Read the problem carefully and solve. Show your work under each question.

A sports team gave away 8,952 t-shirts at a recent home game. There were 14,560 fans at the game. At the next home game, the team gave away water bottles to 7,821 people. There were 15,322 fans at that game.

5. At the game where free t-shirts were given away, how many fans did not receive a free t-shirt? Use a number line to show your work.

6. Out of the fans who did not get a t-shirt, 1,966 of them complained. How many did not complain? Draw a model to show your work.

7. Round the answer to the nearest hundred: _____

8. Compare the number of T-shirts and water bottles given away. Use **<**, **>** or **=** to show which one was greater.

Mid-Test Chapters 1–3

Read the problem carefully and solve. Show your work under each question.

Mr. Foster's Art Shop is ordering art supplies. Mr. Foster orders 36 boxes of paintbrushes. Each box holds 42 paintbrushes. Drawing pencils come in boxes of 213, and Mr. Foster orders 27 boxes. He also orders 8 boxes of colored pencils, and 19 colored pencils come in each box.

9. How many paintbrushes does Mr. Foster order? Use the traditional method to show your work.

10. Write your answer in number name form:

   _____

11. Mr. Foster plans to have a sale on drawing pencils. How many drawing pencils does he order in all? Use the grid method to show your work.

12. Round your answer to the nearest thousand: _____

Mid-Test Chapters 1–3

Read the problem carefully and solve. Show your work under each question.

Anton works at a paper warehouse. He ships 2 orders by truck. Anton wants to split each order equally among trucks. The first order contains 932 boxes of drawing paper. The second order contains 1,460 boxes of cardstock.

13. There are 8 trucks available to ship the order of drawing paper. How many boxes will Anton put on each truck? Solve using the partial quotients method.

14. There are only 2 trucks left to deliver the cardstock. How many boxes will Anton put on each truck? Solve using long division.

15. The second truck is scheduled to make 5 delivery stops. How many boxes of cardstock will each stop receive if the boxes are split equally? Solve using short division.

Check What You Know

Fractions and Decimals

1. $\frac{1}{4}$ + _____ = $\frac{2}{4}$

2. Write an equivalent fraction for $\frac{2}{4}$.

_____

3. _____ − $\frac{1}{9}$ = $\frac{7}{9}$

4. Write an equivalent fraction for $\frac{7}{9}$.

_____

5. Draw a picture to show the answers for #1 and #3. Then, write **>**, **<** or **=** to compare the fractions.

Answer the questions. Show your work.

6. Westberg Bookstore received $\frac{2}{6}$ of its book order. The next day, it received $\frac{1}{6}$ of its book order. How much of the book order does the bookstore have?

7. How much more of the book order does the bookstore have left to receive?

 **Check What You Know**

Fractions and Decimals

Add. Show your work.

8. $6\frac{4}{11}$
   $+1\frac{3}{11}$

9. $8\frac{11}{12}$
   $-1\frac{7}{12}$

10. Amber is making 4 necklaces. Each necklace needs $\frac{6}{8}$ yard of string. How much string does Amber need for all 4 necklaces? Write the addition equation and the multiplication equation for each fraction. Then, solve. Write your answer in simplest form.

11. Emily's plant grew $\frac{2}{10}$ of a centimeter. Justin's plant grew $\frac{40}{100}$ of a centimeter. How many centimeters did the plants grow in all? How can this be shown in a model? How can this be written as a decimal?

Lesson 4.1 Equivalent Fractions

Follow the directions and answer the questions.

Multiply the numerator and the denominator by 6 to find an equivalent fraction.

$\frac{1}{3} =$ _____

Divide the numerator and the denominator by 5 to find an equivalent fraction.

$\frac{10}{15} =$ _____

Use multiplication to find an equivalent fraction.

$\frac{2}{4} = \frac{8}{\boxed{}}$

Use division to find an equivalent fraction.

$\frac{15}{25} = \frac{3}{\boxed{}}$

Jimmy has 24 diamonds. If $\frac{2}{8}$ of the diamonds are yellow, how many yellow diamonds does Jimmy have?

Lesson 4.2 · Comparing Fractions

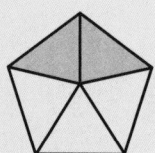 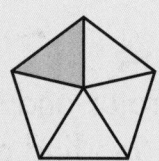

$$\frac{2}{5} > \frac{1}{5}$$

$\frac{2}{5}$ is greater than $\frac{1}{5}$.

 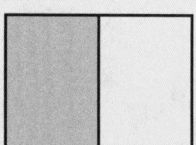

$$\frac{1}{3} < \frac{1}{2}$$

$\frac{1}{3}$ is less than $\frac{1}{2}$.

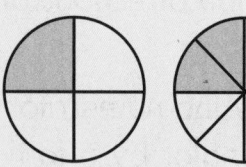

$$\frac{1}{4} = \frac{2}{8} = \frac{2 \times 1}{2 \times 4}$$

$\frac{1}{4}$ is equal to $\frac{2}{8}$.

Draw a picture for each fraction. Then, write **>**, **<**, or **=** to compare the fractions.

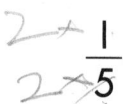 $\frac{2 \times 1}{2 \times 5}$ (=) $\frac{2}{10} = \frac{2 \times 1}{2 \times 5}$

$\frac{3}{4}$ (>) $\frac{1 \times 2}{2 \times 2} = \frac{2}{4}$

India and Hunter are making banners to carry in the town parade. India has finished $\frac{2}{8}$ of her banner, and Hunter has finished $\frac{1}{4}$ of his banner. Draw a picture for each fraction. Then, write **>**, **<**, or **=** to compare the fractions.

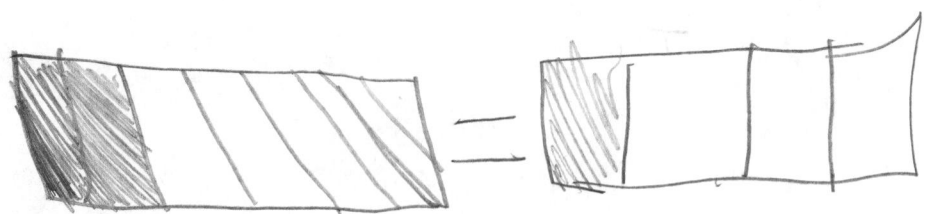

Lesson 4.2   Comparing Fractions

To compare fractions without pictures, the denominators must be the same. When you have unlike denominators, find the **least common multiple (LCM)** and rename the fractions.

$\frac{1}{7 \times 3}$ ◯ $\frac{2}{3 \times 7}$ In the example, the denominators are 3 and 7, so find the LCM of 3 and 7.

$\frac{1 \times 3}{7 \times 3} = \frac{3}{21}$ Multiples of 3: 3, 6, 9, 12, 15, 18, ㉑, 24
   Multiples of 7: 7, 14, ㉑, 28

$\frac{2 \times 7}{3 \times 7} = \frac{14}{21}$ The least common multiple of 3 and 7 is 21. To change each fraction so it has the same denominator, multiply both the numerator and denominator by the same number. Look at the

$\frac{3}{21}$ $<$ $\frac{14}{21}$ numerator to determine the larger fraction.

For each fraction pair, write equivalent fractions with a common denominator. Then, compare the fractions.

$\frac{4}{8}$ ◯ $\frac{2}{10}$ $\frac{3}{12}$ ◯ $\frac{1}{3}$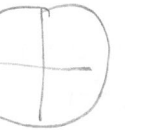

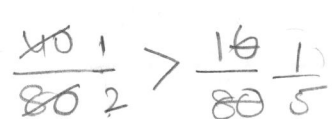 $\frac{40}{80}\frac{1}{2} > \frac{16}{80}\frac{1}{5}$ 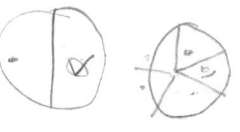 $\frac{3 \times 3}{12 \times 3}$ $\frac{1 \times 12}{3 \times 12}$

$\frac{9}{36}\frac{1}{4} < \frac{12}{36}\frac{1}{3}$

Morgan says that $\frac{2}{4}$ is the same as $\frac{8}{16}$, but Pilar says it is the same as $\frac{1}{2}$. Who is correct? Why?

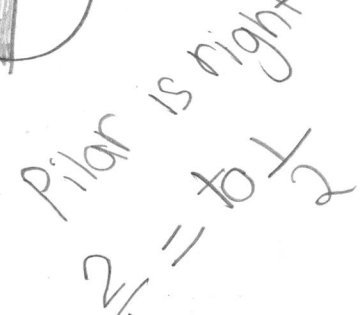

Pilar is right because $\frac{2}{4} = \frac{1}{2}$

Lesson 4.3 Adding Fractions with Like Denominators

$$\frac{2}{8} + \frac{5}{8} = \frac{7}{8} \quad or \quad \frac{2}{8} + \frac{5}{8} = \frac{2+5}{8} = \frac{7}{8}$$

Add the numerators. Write the sum over the common denominator.

Draw a picture to solve.

$$\frac{2}{7} + \frac{2}{7} = \frac{4}{7}$$

Add. Show your work.

Madison completes $\frac{2}{8}$ of her math homework before dance class. After dance class, she completes $\frac{4}{8}$ more. How much of her math homework has Madison finished?

$$\frac{4}{8} \frac{2}{8} = \frac{6}{8}$$

she finished $\frac{6}{8}$ of her math homework

Madison has enough time before school the next morning to do $\frac{1}{8}$ more of her math homework. How much of her homework is still not finished?

$$\frac{7}{8}$$

she has to do $\frac{7}{8}$ of her homework

Lesson 4.4   Subtracting Fractions with Like Denominators

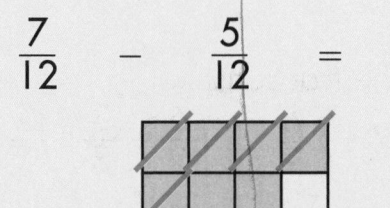

$$\frac{7}{12} - \frac{5}{12} = \frac{2}{12}$$ or $$\frac{7}{12} - \frac{5}{12} = \frac{7-5}{12} = \frac{2}{12}$$

Subtract the numerators. Write the difference over the common denominator.

Draw a picture to subtract.

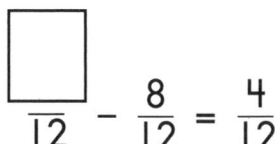

$$\frac{\boxed{}}{12} - \frac{8}{12} = \frac{4}{12}$$

Subtract. Show your work.

Ethan and Carson both decide to walk down the wooded path. After walking $\frac{7}{10}$ of the way, the boys stop to watch an eagle fly by. How far do they have left to walk? Write your subtraction sentence.

Lesson 4.5 Adding Mixed Numbers

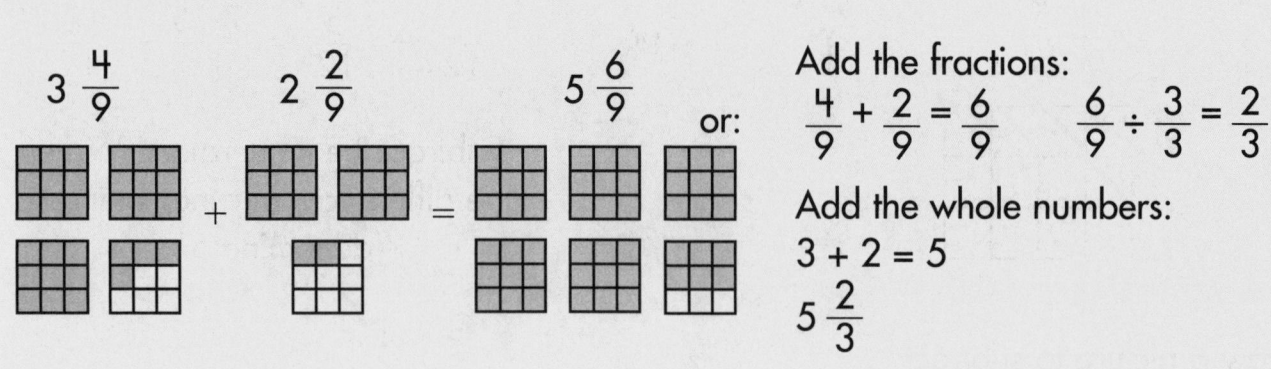

$$3\frac{4}{9} \qquad 2\frac{2}{9} \qquad 5\frac{6}{9} \quad \text{or:}$$

Add the fractions:
$$\frac{4}{9} + \frac{2}{9} = \frac{6}{9} \qquad \frac{6}{9} \div \frac{3}{3} = \frac{2}{3}$$

Add the whole numbers:
$$3 + 2 = 5$$
$$5\frac{2}{3}$$

Draw pictures to add.

$$5\frac{3}{8} \quad + \quad 8\frac{3}{8} \quad = \quad \underline{\hspace{2cm}}$$

Heather gets 2 packages in the mail. One weighs $2\frac{2}{9}$ pounds, and the other weighs $7\frac{2}{9}$ pounds. What is the weight of the 2 packages?

The next day, Heather gets a third package that weighs $2\frac{2}{9}$ pounds. What is the weight of all 3 packages?

Lesson 4.6 Subtracting Mixed Numbers

$$3\frac{2}{8} \;-\; 1\frac{2}{8} \;=\; 2\frac{1}{8} \quad \text{or:}$$

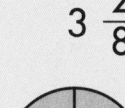

Subtract the fractions:

$$\frac{3}{8} - \frac{2}{8} = \frac{1}{8} \qquad \frac{6}{9} \div \frac{3}{3} = \frac{2}{3}$$

Add the whole numbers:

$$3 - 1 = 2$$

$$2\frac{1}{8}$$

Draw pictures to subtract.

$$7\frac{9}{10} \;-\; 2\frac{3}{10} \;=\; \underline{\quad\quad}$$

Alexis has 2 kittens. The orange tabby weighs $9\frac{3}{7}$ pounds. The gray tabby weighs $7\frac{2}{7}$ pounds. How much more does the orange tabby weigh than the gray tabby?

Lesson 4.7 Decomposing Fractions

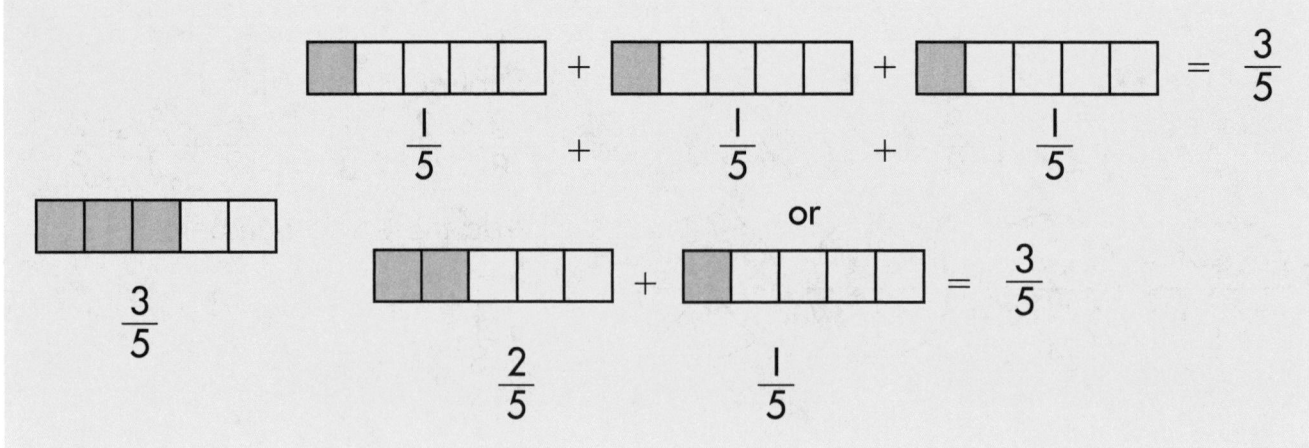

Decompose each fraction in 2 ways. Write 2 equations to show your thinking.

$\dfrac{5}{6}$

Samantha has $\dfrac{3}{4}$ of a cherry pie left. How can she divide the cherry pie to store it in the refrigerator? Show 2 ways to decompose the pie. Draw a picture and write the equations to show your thinking.

Lesson 4.8 Fractions as Multiples

Fractions can be shown as muliplication equations and addition equations.

$$\frac{4}{5} = 4 \times \left(\frac{1}{5}\right) \qquad \frac{1}{5} + \frac{1}{5} + \frac{1}{5} + \frac{1}{5} = \frac{4}{5}$$

Write the addition equation and the multiplication equation for each fraction.

$\dfrac{3}{4}$ $\dfrac{5}{7}$

April has 5 exercises in her exercise routine. She does each exercise for $\frac{1}{6}$ of an hour. How long is April's exercise routine? Write the addition equation and the multiplication equation for the fraction. Then, solve.

Lesson 4.9   Multiplying Fractions and Whole Numbers

$\frac{2}{3} \times 6 = \frac{2}{3} \times \frac{6}{1}$ Rewrite the whole number as a fraction. $7 \times \frac{1}{2} = \frac{7}{1} \times \frac{1}{2}$

$\quad = \frac{2 \times 6}{3 \times 1}$ Multiply the numerators. $\quad = \frac{7 \times 1}{1 \times 2}$
    Multiply the denominators.

$\quad = \frac{12}{3}$ $\quad = \frac{7}{2}$

$\quad = 4$ Reduce to simplest form. $\quad = 3\frac{1}{2}$

Multiply. Write answers in simplest form.

$\frac{1}{2} \times 5$ $7 \times \frac{3}{4}$

One serving of pancakes calls for $\frac{2}{3}$ cup of milk. One serving of waffles calls for $\frac{1}{3}$ cup of milk. Brad wants to make 5 servings of waffles and 5 servings of pancakes. How many cups of milk will Brad need altogether?

Lesson 4.9   Multiplying Fractions and Whole Numbers

Write a word problem that goes with the problem given. Solve. Write your answers in simplest form.

$\dfrac{5}{9} \times 7 =$

_____

_____

_____

_____

_____

_____

Solve the problem. Write your answer in simplest form.

$2 \times \dfrac{3}{4} =$

Lesson 4.10 Understanding Decimals to Hundredths

The fraction $\frac{4}{10}$ is the same as the decimal 0.4. The fraction $\frac{45}{100}$ is the same as the decimal 0.45.

The first two place values to the right of the decimal point are tenths and hundredths. The fraction $\frac{45}{100}$ can be broken down into $\frac{40}{100} + \frac{5}{100}$ to show the tenths (4) and hundredths (5) digits.

Look at the addition problem below with fractions and decimals.

$$\frac{4}{10} + \frac{5}{100} = \frac{40}{100} + \frac{5}{100} = \frac{45}{100}$$

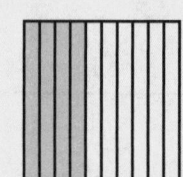 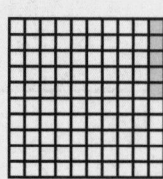 

0.40 + 0.05 = 0.45

Find the number of tenths or hundredths in the model. Write the total as a fraction and as a decimal.

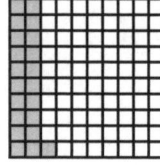

Draw a model for the fraction given. Then, write the total as a decimal.

$$\frac{84}{100}$$

Fraction: _____ Decimal: _____

Decimal: _____

NAME _____

Check What You Learned

Fractions and Decimals

Read carefully and solve. Show your work under each question.

A group of friends went to the movies. In the lobby, $\frac{4}{10}$ of the group decided to see a comedy and $\frac{5}{10}$ decided to see a drama.

1. How much larger is the fraction of the group that decided to see a drama?

2. What fraction of the group decided to see something other than a drama or comedy?

3. Using **>**, **<**, or **=**, compare the fraction of the group that wanted to see a comedy to the fraction that wanted to see a drama.

4. It takes Scott $5\frac{3}{8}$ days to make a birdhouse and $8\frac{3}{8}$ days to make a picnic table. How many days will it take Scott to make both the birdhouse and the picnic table? Draw a model to show your work.

CHAPTER 4 POSTTEST

 **Check What You Learned**

Fractions and Decimals

Solve.

5. Mario swims at the neighborhood swimming pool for $\frac{6}{9}$ of an hour 2 times a week. How many total hours does Mario swim each week? Write the addition and multiplication equation for the fraction. Then, solve. Write in simplest form.

6. A single serving of gelatin dessert requires $\frac{3}{4}$ cup of sugar. How much sugar is needed for 7 servings? How much more sugar would be needed for 10 servings of gelatin dessert?

8. Draw a model for the fraction given. Then, write the total as a decimal.

$\frac{37}{100}$

Check What You Know

Measurement

Read carefully and solve. Show your work under each problem.

The Taylor family is ordering food and drinks for the family reunion party. They order a 95-inch turkey and cheese sub from the local deli. They also buy 7 gallons of lemonade.

1. About how many feet long is the turkey and cheese sub?

2. The Taylor family is expecting 28 total people at the reunion. How many cups of lemonade will each person get?

Ian signs up for a fitness competition. First, he must carry 8 buckets filled with 1,000 mL of water across an empty field. Then, he must lift a 45 kg weight above his head 8 times.

3. After Ian carries the 8 buckets of water, how many liters will he have carried across the field?

4. Ian lifts the weight above his head 5 times. How many total grams has he lifted after the fifth time?

NAME _____

 **Check What You Know**

Measurement

Read carefully and solve. Show your work under each question.

5. Wayne bought a piece of land to build on. It is shaped like a rectangle and has a perimeter of 120 yards. One side of the property is 20 yards long. What is the area of the property?

6. Use a protractor to measure the angle shown.

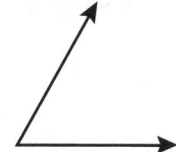

7. How many more degrees would you need to measure to equal 180°? Draw that angle.

8. A group of geologists measured the angles of some cliffs in the Rocky Mountains. Display the data on a line plot.

Angle Measurements of Cliffs in the Rocky Mountains	
45°	ⅢⅢ
46°	‖‖‖‖
47°	ⅢⅢ ‖‖‖‖
48°	‖‖‖
49°	‖‖

Lesson 5.1 Units of Length (Standard)

Helpful Hint

1 foot (ft.) = 12 inches (in.)
1 yard (yd.) = 3 feet (ft.) = 36 inches (in.)

1 mile (mi.) = 1,760 yards (yd.)
= 5,280 feet (ft.)

27 feet = _____ inches
Feet is larger than inches, so you would multiply.

When converting from a larger unit to a smaller unit, multiply. When converting from a smaller unit to a larger unit, divide.

There are 12 inches in a foot, so 12 x 27 is your expression.
There are 324 inches in 27 feet.

Answer the questions. Write the equation you used to show your work.

48 in. = _____ ft.

7 mi. = _____ yd.

Becky and Ansley buy fabric at the store to make clothing. They buy brown and green fabric. Becky buys 6 feet of green fabric. Ansley buys 107 inches of brown fabric. How many more inches of fabric does Ansley buy than Becky?

Lesson 5.2   Units of Length (Metric)

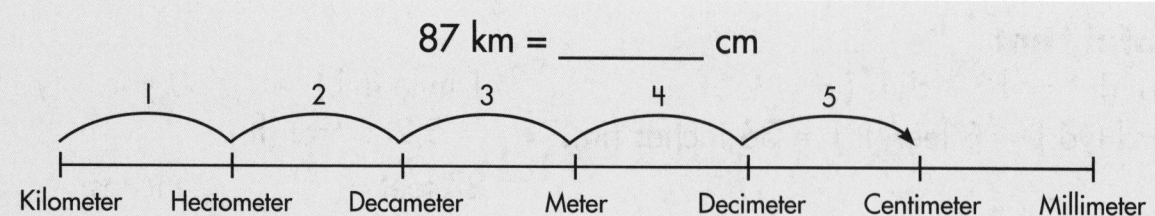

87 km = _____ cm

87.00000   Move the decimal 5 places to the right, adding zeros as you go.
  1 2 3 4 5

8,700,000 cm

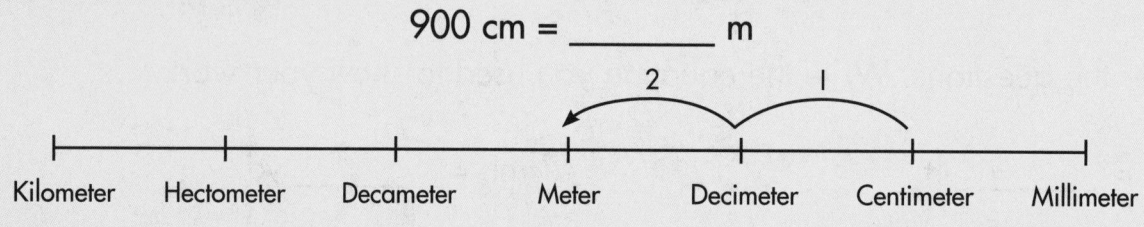

900 cm = _____ m

9.00   Move the decimal 2 places to the left.
 2 1

9 meters

Complete the conversions. Draw a number line to show your work.

Centimeters	Meters	Kilometers
600,000		
		2
	3,000	

Lesson 5.3 Liquid Volume (Standard)

Conversion Table

1 cup (c.) = 8 ounces (oz.)

1 pint (pt.) = 2 cups (c.)

1 quart (qt.) = 2 pints (pt.)

1 quart (qt.) = 4 cups (c.)

1 gallon (gal.) = 4 quarts (qt.)

1 gallon (gal.) = 8 pints (pt.)

1 gallon (gal.) = 16 cups (c.)

When converting from a larger unit to a smaller unit, multiply.

7 qt. = _____ pt.

1 qt. = 2 pt.

$7 \times 2 = 14$

7 qt. = 14 pt.

When converting from a smaller unit to a larger unit, divide.

16 qt. = _____ gal.

4 qt. = 1 gal.

$16 \div 4 = 4$

16 qt. = 4 gal.

Solve the problems. Show your work.

80 qt. = _____ pt.

18 c. = _____ pt.

28 qt. = _____ gal.

64 oz. = _____ c.

Lesson 5.4 Liquid Volume (Metric)

12 L = _____ mL

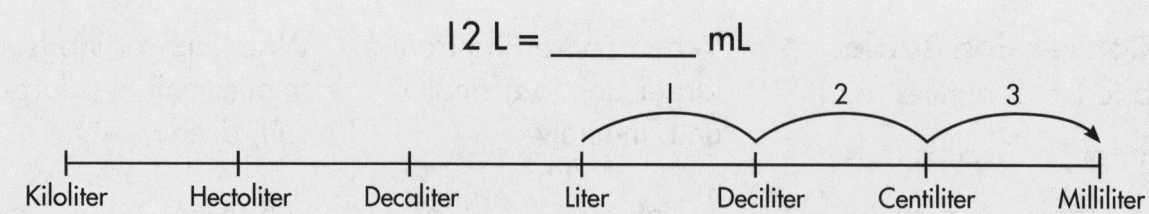

12,000   Move the decimal 3 places to the right, adding zeros as you go.
  1 2 3

12,000 mL

2,500 mL = _____ L

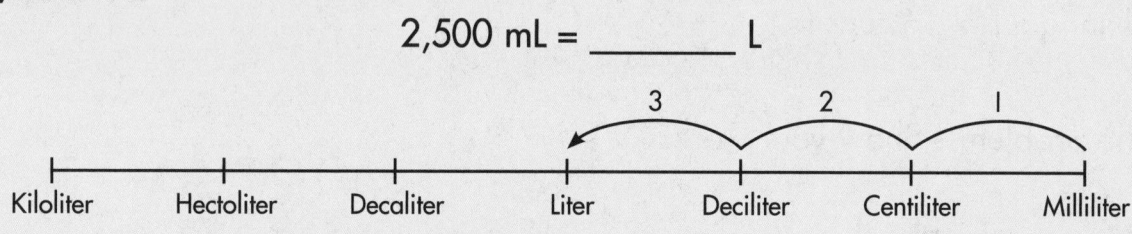

2,500   Move the decimal 3 places to the left.
  3 2 1

Move the **decimal** to the left on the number line as many times as you jump.
Start at **milliliter** and move as many jumps to the left as it takes to get to **liter.**
It takes 3 jumps. So, move the decimal 3 places to the left.

2.5 liters

Complete the conversions. Draw a number line to show your work.

3 L = _____ mL

5,400 mL = _____ L

The doggie daycare center has pools for the dogs to play in. One pool holds 75
liters of water. The other pool holds 100 liters of water. How many milliliters of water
do the 2 pools hold altogether?

Lesson 5.5 Weight (Standard)

Conversion Table

$\frac{1}{2}$ pound (lb.) = 8 ounces (oz.)

1 pound (lb.) = 16 ounces (oz.)

$\frac{1}{2}$ ton (T.) = 1,000 pounds (lb.)

1 ton (T.) = 2,000 pounds (lb.)

When converting from a larger unit to a smaller unit, multiply.

5 lb. = _____ oz.

1 lb. = 16 oz.
5 × 16 = 80
5 lb. = 80 oz.

When converting from a smaller unit to a larger unit, divide.

6,000 lb. = _____ T.

2,000 lb. = 1 T.
6,000 ÷ 2,000 = 3
6,000 lb. = 3 T.

Complete the table.

Tons	Pounds	Ounces
8		256,000
	8,000	
6		
5		
		288,000

Answer the questions. Show your work.

Blair visits the zoo with his family. He learns that the male African elephant weighs 6 tons. He learns that the female African elephant weighs 4,000 pounds. How many more pounds does the male weigh than the female?

Lesson 5.6   Weight (Metric)

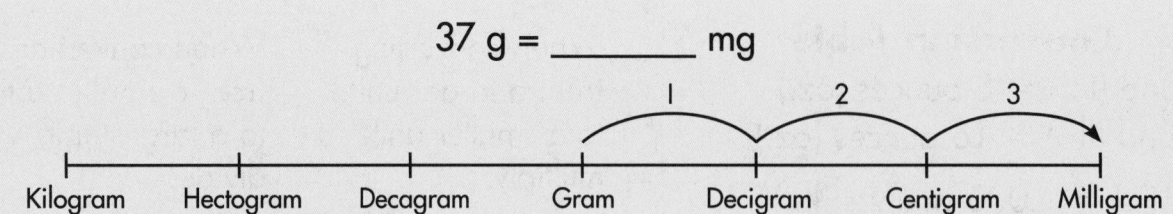

37 g = _____ mg

37.000.
  1 2 3
Move the decimal 3 places to the right, adding zeros as you go.

37,000 mg

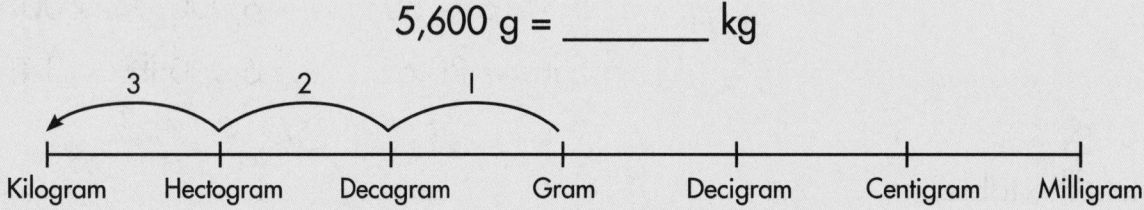

5,600 g = _____ kg

5.600.
3 2 1
Move the decimal 3 places to the left.

5.6 kg

Complete the conversions. Draw a number line to show your work.

183 kg = _____ g

37 g = _____ mg

Monica packed 3 bags to take with her on vacation. One bag weighed 20,000 g, one weighed 12,000 g, and the third one weighed 5,000 g. How many kilograms do the bags weigh altogether?

Lesson 5.7   Measuring Perimeter

Perimeter is the distance around a shape. To find the perimeter, add together the lengths of all the sides of a figure.

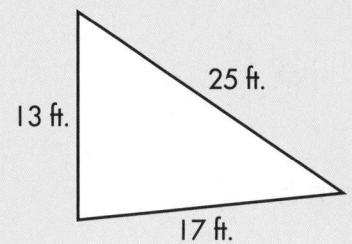

$13 + 25 + 17 = 55$

The perimeter of this triangle is 55 feet.

Draw a rectangle with a perimeter of 34 units.

Draw a rectangle with a perimeter of 20 units.

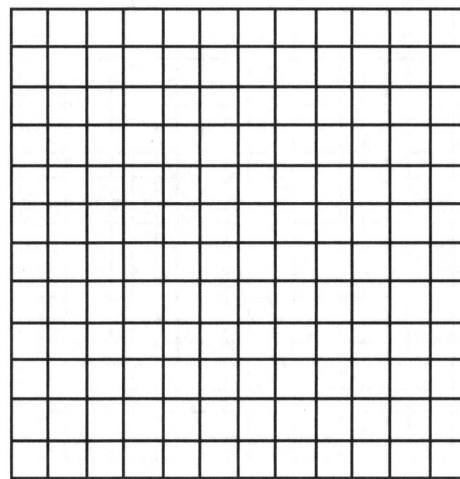

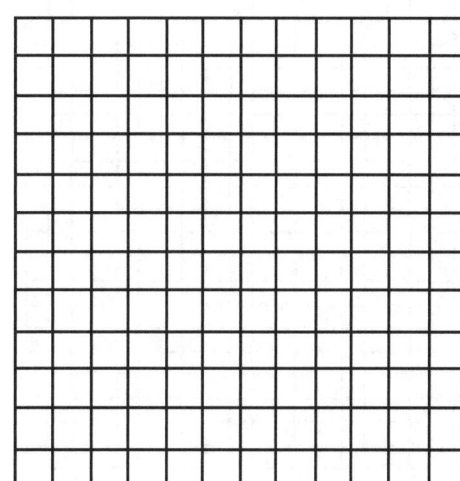

Parker cleared a vacant rectangle-shaped lot to plant a garden. The perimeter of the lot was 100 feet. If one side measured 15 feet, what were the measurements of the other 3 sides of the lot?

Lesson 5.8 Measuring Area

Area is the amount of space a shape covers. To find the area of a square or rectangle, multiply length by width.

100 ft. (length)

20 ft. (width)

$A = 100 \text{ ft.} \times 20 \text{ ft.} = 2,000 \text{ sq. ft.}$

Draw a square with an area of 224 sq. units.

Draw a rectangle with an area of 54 sq. units.

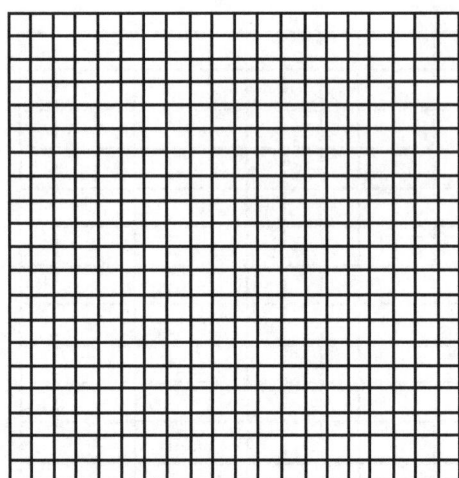

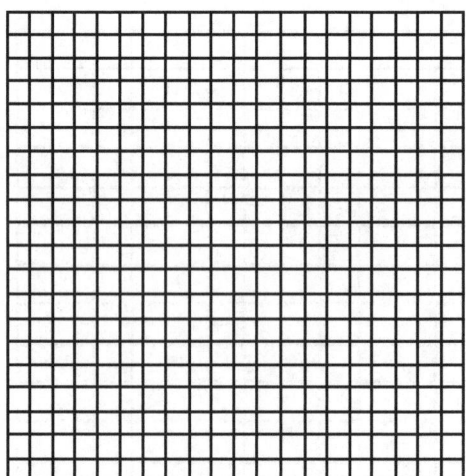

Michelle is covering the floor in a room with an area of 600 square feet. The room is 20 feet wide. How long is the room?

Lesson 5.9　Measurement Line Plots

A line plot is a graph that shows the frequency of data occurring along a number line.

A group of students measured the lengths of books on a shelf to the nearest $\frac{1}{2}$ inch. The numbers of books measuring each length are shown in the chart.

To show data on a line plot, draw a number line. Then, label the different lengths on the number line. Last, count the number of times each length was counted. Draw X's above each length to show how many times each one was counted.

Lengths of Books on a Shelf in Inches	
4	卌
$4\frac{1}{2}$	卌 I
5	I
$5\frac{1}{2}$	III
6	II
$6\frac{1}{2}$	卌

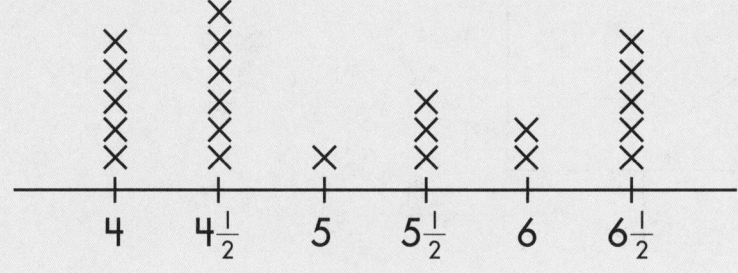

Complete the line plot for the data given.

A baker counted the number of cups of sugar she used when making different kinds of cookies. Show the data on the line plot.

Cups of Sugar Used in Cookies	
2	卌 II
$2\frac{1}{2}$	卌 I
3	IIII
$3\frac{1}{2}$	II
4	I
$4\frac{1}{2}$	I

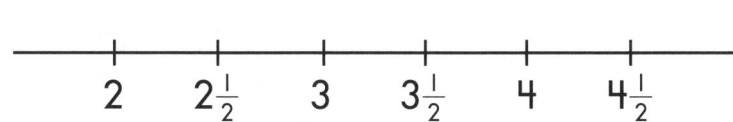

Lesson 5.10   Measuring and Drawing Angles

A protractor is used to measure an angle. The angle is measured in degrees. The protractor to the right shows a 60-degree angle.

Measure all the angles on the angle character. Write the measurement in the vertex of each angle.

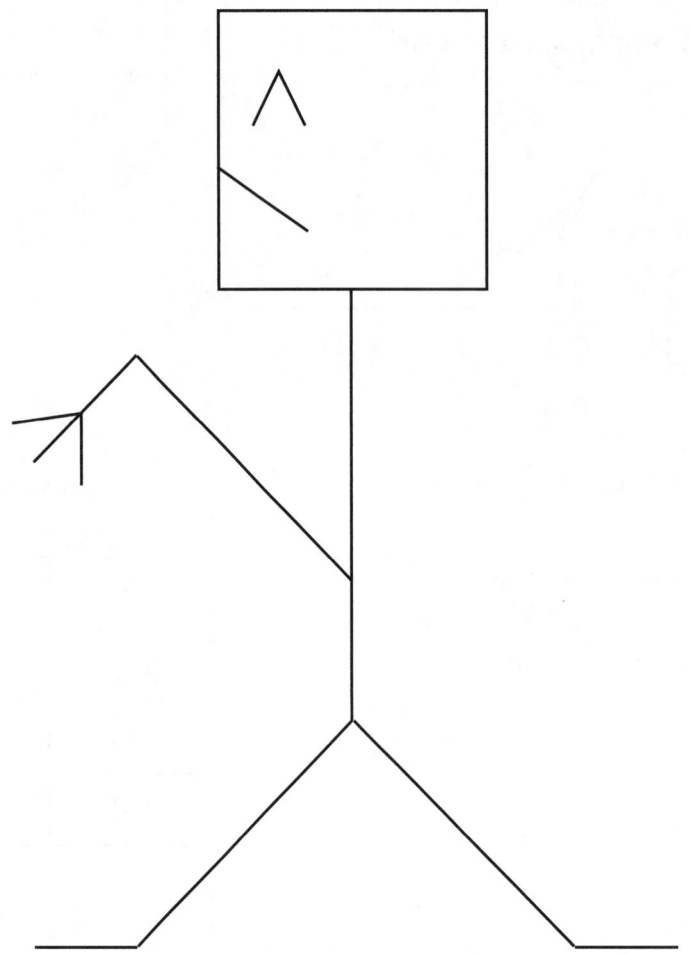

Lesson 5.11 Missing Angles

If the measurement of one angle is known, the measurement of the other angle can be found. If 2 angles measure 90°, 180°, 270°, or 360°, the measure of one angle can be used to find the measure of the other.

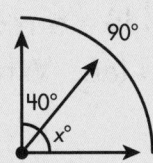
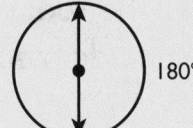
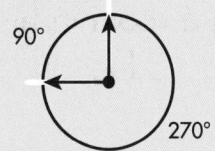
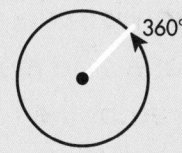

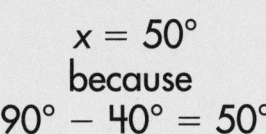

$x = 50°$
because
$90° - 40° = 50°$

A 360° rotation about a point makes a complete circle.

A water sprinkler covers 75° of a lawn. How many more degrees would it need to cover in order to water 180° of the lawn?

At the ice skating rink, Mackenzie tries to do a 360° turn. She only makes it 187°. How many degrees short of her goal was she?

Brian is building a birdhouse. He rotates it 132° clockwise. Then, he rotates it another 95° clockwise. How many more degrees does Brian need to rotate the birdhouse to make a 290° turn?

 **Check What You Learned**

Measurement

Read carefully and solve. Show your work under each question.

1. Dawson is redecorating a room in his house. The room is shaped like a rectangle, with one side measuring 15 feet and the other side measuring 20 feet. What is the area of the room?

2. Meteorologists across the globe measured rainfall over 7 days. Display the data on the line plot.

Inches of Rainfall Over 7 Days	
2	| | | |
3	| | |
4	| |
5	|

```
 ───┼────┼────┼────┼───
    2    3    4    5
```

3. At 12:20 AM, the measurement between the short hand and the big hand on the clock is 114°. How many more degrees would give an angle measurement of 245°?

 # Check What You Learned

Measurement

Read each problem carefully and solve. Show your work under each problem.

Sasha exercises every day after school. First, she runs 5 miles. Then, she lifts 80 pounds of weight with her arms, and 120 pounds of weight with her legs.

4. How many yards does Sasha run every day after school?

5. How many ounces of weight does she lift with her arms and legs combined?

Mrs. Murphy works in a local bakery. Early every morning, she prepares 15 meters of French bread dough, and 30 grams of cinnamon and sugar sprinkle.

6. How many centimeters of French bread dough does Mrs. Murphy prepare each morning?

7. How many milligrams of cinnamon and sugar sprinkle does she prepare?

NAME _____

Check What You Know

Geometry

Mariah draws a map of her neighborhood. She lives on Apple Street. Orange Street and Banana Street are both parallel to Mariah's street. Carrot Avenue and Cucumber Avenue are both perpendicular to her street. The library is on Cucumber Avenue. Mariah's best friend, Abbie, lives on Orange Street.

1. Draw a map of Mariah's neighborhood according to the directions given.

2. In your answer to question #1, draw a ray, starting at Mariah's house, pointing to the library. Then, draw another ray starting at Mariah's house, pointing to Abbie's house.

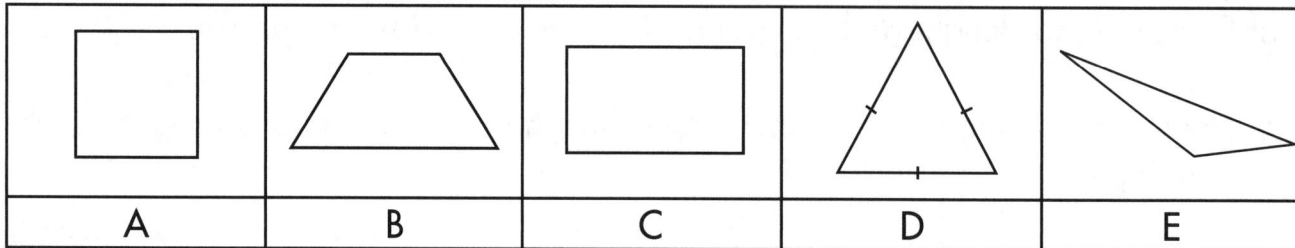

3. Write the name of each shape above.

A = _____   B = _____

C = _____   D = _____

E = _____

Lesson 6.1 Points, Lines, Rays, Angles

A **point** is an exact location in space.
A **line** goes in both directions with no endpoints.
A **line segment** is part of a line. It has two endpoints.
A **ray** is a line that has one endpoint. It continues on and on in one direction.
A **vertex** is a point formed by two rays sharing a common endpoint.

Identify the rays and vertex of the angle.

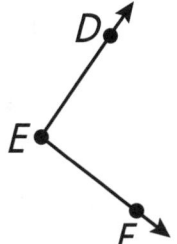

rays: _____   _____

vertex: _____

angle: _____

Nicole drew an angle with a vertex of *Y* and rays labeled *YZ* and *YX*. Draw the angle that Nicole drew below and label the rays and vertex.

Owen draws a line on his paper. Norris draws a line segment on his paper. Owen says they are the same, but Norris says they are different. Draw what Owen drew and what Norris drew. Who is correct?

Lesson 6.2   Parallel and Perpendicular Lines

Parallel lines never intersect, or cross over, each other. They are always the same distance apart.
Intersecting lines cross over each other.
Perpendicular lines intersect each other to form right angles.

Leo draws a map of the streets near his school. He uses parallel lines, intersecting lines, and perpendicular lines to show how the streets look in the area.

Water Street and Ortiz Avenue are perpendicular to each other on the map. Draw what Water Street and Ortiz Avenue look like on the map.

Virginia Way and 3rd Avenue are parallel to each other, and are also parallel to Front Street. Draw what all three of these streets would look like on the map.

Magnolia Manor intersects with Virginia Way, 3rd Avenue and Front Street. However, it is **not** perpendicular to any of them. Draw what this would look like on Leo's map.

Lesson 6.3 Symmetrical Shapes

Use the grid lines to help you draw the mirror image of the flower.

Lesson 6.4   Quadrilaterals

A **quadrilateral** is a polygon with 4 sides. Here are some examples:

parallelogram – a quadrilateral with opposite sides parallel

square – rectangle with 4 sides of the same length and all angles equal

rectangle – parallelogram with 4 right angles. Opposite sides are equal.

rhombus – parallelogram with all 4 sides the same length. Opposite angles are the same measure.

kite – 2 pairs of adjacent sides that are congruent

trapezoid – only 2 sides are parallel

Beth made a sign in the shape of a trapezoid. What did her sign look like? Draw it below.

Abigail is playing a game with her friends. She describes something, and they must guess what it is she is describing. She says, "This object has 4 sides all the same length, and 4 angles that each measure 90°." One friend says it's a square, and one friend says it's a parallelogram. Who is correct? Explain your thinking.

_____

_____

_____

_____

Lesson 6.5 Triangles

A **triangle** is a polygon with 3 sides. Here are some examples:

scalene triangle – all 3 sides have different lengths. Each angle is also different.

isosceles triangle – 2 sides have equal lengths; 2 angles are also equal

equilateral triangle – all 3 sides are the same length, and all 3 angles equal 60°

acute triangle – all angles are less than 90°

right triangle – has 1 right angle

obtuse triangle – 1 angle that measures more than 90°

Can an obtuse triangle ever be an acute triangle? How do you know?

_____

_____

_____

Shane described a triangle as having a right angle and 2 other angles measuring 45°. What 2 kinds of triangles could Shane be describing? How do you know?

_____

_____

_____

Lesson 6.6   Geometric Patterns

What are the next 2 objects in this pattern?

This is an A-A-B pattern.

Cross out the object that is not in the correct sequence.

What should be there instead?

The object should be a hexagon.

This is an A-B-C-D pattern.

Draw the next 2 objects in each pattern.

Find the object that is out of sequence. Cross it out. Draw the correct object on the blank line.

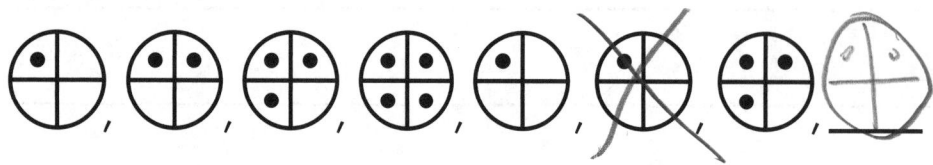

Create your own A-A-B-B pattern. Draw it below.

Lesson 6.6 Geometric Patterns

Felicia, Jay, and Holly each created geometric patterns out of these 4 shapes.

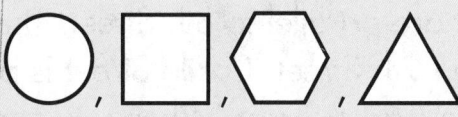

Felicia created an A-A-B pattern. Draw 2 different patterns she could make. Label each pattern set.

Jay created an A-B-B-A pattern. Draw 2 different patterns he could make. Label each pattern set.

Holly created an A-B-C-D pattern. Draw 2 different patterns she could make. Label each pattern set.

Check What You Learned

Geometry

Miranda draws a map of all of her favorite places in town. The bookstore is on 8th Street. 9th and 10th Street are parallel to 8th Street. The pet store is on 10th Street and the candy store is on 9th Street. Castle Street is perpendicular to all 3 of the other streets. The park is on Castle Street. When you connect the points of the bookstore, the pet store, and the candy store, and use the bookstore as the vertex, you should see an acute angle.

1. Draw a map of all of Miranda's favorite places. Use a point to label each place. Draw the angle described.

2. Create a pattern using an equilateral triangle, a parallelogram, a rhombus, and a right triangle. Label the pattern set after you draw it.

Final Test Chapters 1–6

In Allen County, there are 4 different high schools, each with its own football team. Each team collected clothes to send to the American Red Cross to help victims of natural disasters. The chart shows what each team sent.

Football Teams	Pounds of Clothes
Parkside High	489
Winterville High	1,578
Forrest Lane High	369
Blakely High	4,875

1. How many pounds of clothing did Parkside High and Winterville High send altogether? Use models to show your work.

2. How many more pounds of clothing did Blakely High collect than Winterville High? Use a number line to show your work.

3. Write both totals above in expanded form. Then, round both totals to the nearest thousand.

Final Test Chapters 1–6

Solve the problems.

4. The cafeteria planned to bake 3 chocolate chip cookies for every student in the school. If there are 3,114 students, how many cookies does the cafeteria need to bake? Use the grid method to show your work.

5. In the past 8 weeks, Iman worked on 504 computers. Each week, he worked on the same number of computers. How many computers did he work on every week? Use the partial quotients method to show your work.

6. Mrs. Garcia checked how much time her students spend doing homework. If each of her 32 students spends 18 hours each week, how much homework do the students do in a week? Use the traditional method to show your work.

Final Test Chapters 1–6

Solve the problems.

7. Logan scored 234 points this season playing basketball. He played in 9 games and scored the same number of points in each game. How many points did he score in each game? Use long division to show your work.

8. Logan's brother Mason scored 253 points this season. How many points did Logan and Mason score altogether this season? Use a number line to show your work.

9. At baseball practice, 1,512 pitches were thrown. If 6 players received the same number of pitches, how many pitches did each player receive? Use short division to show your work.

Final Test Chapters 1–6

On Monday, Kayla spends $3\frac{2}{6}$ hours writing a story. She takes a break and then continues working for another $5\frac{3}{6}$ hours. Use this information to solve problems 10 and 11.

10. How many total hours does Kayla spend writing her story on Monday?

11. How many more hours does she spend writing after her break than before it?

12. Libby takes her dog to the dog park for $\frac{3}{9}$ of an hour 4 times a week. How many total hours does Libby take her dog to the dog park each week? Write the addition equation and multiplication equation. Then, solve.

13. Solve the problem below. Draw a model for the answer. Then, write the answer in decimal form.

$$\frac{35}{100} + \frac{2}{10} =$$

Final Test Chapters 1–6

Ryan runs a catering company. A local radio station has just ordered a lunch to be catered at its studio next week. Their order is as follows:

Baked Ziti	5 pounds
Garlic Bread	3 feet
Iced Tea	4 gallons

Use the table at left to solve problems 14, 15, and 16.

14. How many inches of garlic bread did the radio station order?

15. How many ounces of baked ziti did the radio station order?

16. When Ryan delivered the order to the station, he did not have any gallon containers left for the iced tea, so he had to use pint containers. How many pint containers did Ryan use?

17. William is putting new trim around the perimeter of his dining room and tile on the floor. His dining room is a rectangle, with the long sides measuring 15 meters and the short sides measuring 9 meters. What is the perimeter of the room? What is the area?

Spectrum Critical Thinking for Math
Grade 4

Final Test Chapters 1–6

18. Complete the geometric pattern.

 ____ , ____ , ____ , ____

19. Write the name of the 4 shapes used in the geometric pattern above.

_____   _____   _____   _____

20. A walking club recorded the miles each member walked in a week. Show the data on the line plot.

Number of Miles	Number of Members
5	卌 l
$5\frac{1}{2}$	卌
6	l l l
$6\frac{1}{2}$	l l l

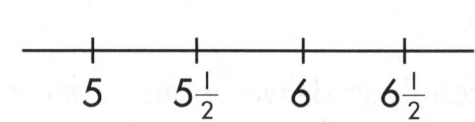

21. Shannon lives on Balsam Ave. Her grandmother lives on Maple Ave. The only way to travel from Shannon's house to her grandmother's is to walk to Winter Street, which is perpendicular to both Balsam Ave. and Maple Ave. Draw a map showing Shannon's street, her grandmother's street, and how she can travel between both streets.

CHAPTERS 1–6 FINAL TEST

Spectrum Critical Thinking for Math
Grade 4
100

Chapters 1–6
Final Test

Answer Key

Page 4

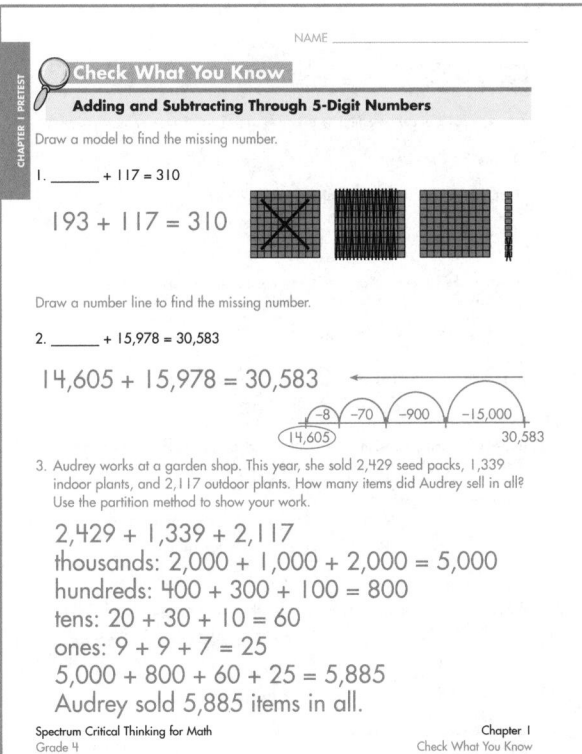

Check What You Know
Adding and Subtracting Through 5-Digit Numbers

Draw a model to find the missing number.

1. _____ + 117 = 310

$193 + 117 = 310$

Draw a number line to find the missing number.

2. _____ + 15,978 = 30,583

$14,605 + 15,978 = 30,583$

−8   −70   −900   −15,000
14,605   30,583

3. Audrey works at a garden shop. This year, she sold 2,429 seed packs, 1,339 indoor plants, and 2,117 outdoor plants. How many items did Audrey sell in all? Use the partition method to show your work.

$2,429 + 1,339 + 2,117$
thousands: $2,000 + 1,000 + 2,000 = 5,000$
hundreds: $400 + 300 + 100 = 800$
tens: $20 + 30 + 10 = 60$
ones: $9 + 9 + 7 = 25$
$5,000 + 800 + 60 + 25 = 5,885$
Audrey sold 5,885 items in all.

Page 5

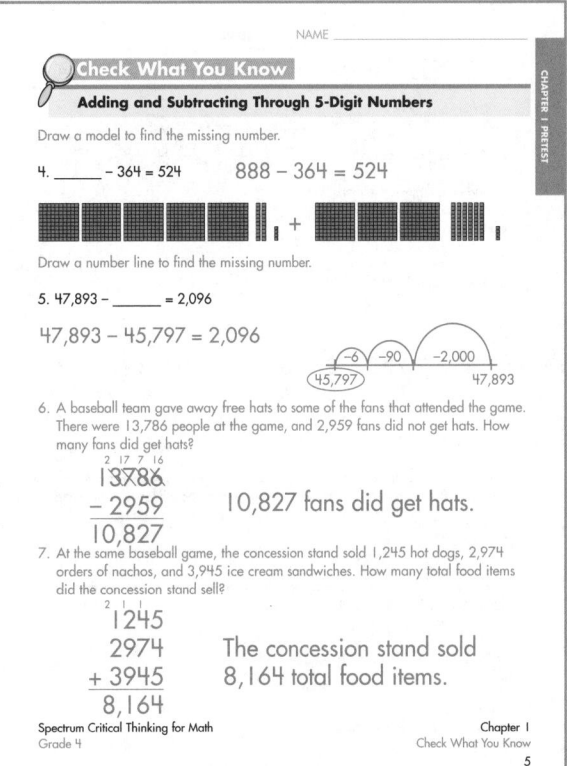

Check What You Know
Adding and Subtracting Through 5-Digit Numbers

Draw a model to find the missing number.

4. _____ − 364 = 524 $888 − 364 = 524$

Draw a number line to find the missing number.

5. 47,893 − _____ = 2,096

$47,893 − 45,797 = 2,096$

−6   −90   −2,000
45,797   47,893

6. A baseball team gave away free hats to some of the fans that attended the game. There were 13,786 people at the game, and 2,959 fans did not get hats. How many fans did get hats?

$\begin{array}{r} 13786 \\ -\ 2959 \\ \hline 10,827 \end{array}$ 10,827 fans did get hats.

7. At the same baseball game, the concession stand sold 1,245 hot dogs, 2,974 orders of nachos, and 3,945 ice cream sandwiches. How many total food items did the concession stand sell?

$\begin{array}{r} 1245 \\ 2974 \\ +\ 3945 \\ \hline 8,164 \end{array}$ The concession stand sold 8,164 total food items.

Page 6

Lesson 1.1 Addition and Subtraction in the Real World

Jackie has 46 stamps in her collection, and Irene has 23 stamps. How many stamps do Jackie and Irene have altogether? Jackie will get 10 more stamps for her birthday. How many stamps will Jackie and Irene have after Jackie's birthday?

First, add what Jackie and Irene have now: $46 + 23 = 69$
Then, add the 10 stamps that Jackie will get for her birthday: $69 + 10 = 79$

Jackie and Irene will have 79 stamps altogether after Jackie's birthday.

Solve. Write the addition or subtraction sentences you used.

Yuri's soccer team is in the State Cup Tournament. There were 78 goals made in the entire tournament. Yuri's team made 29 of the goals. How many goals did the other teams make?

$78 − 29 = 49$ $\begin{array}{r} 78 \\ -\ 29 \\ \hline 49 \end{array}$

The other teams scored 49 goals.

Elena's team scored 16 goals in the tournament. How many goals did Yuri's team and Elena's team score altogether?

$29 + 16 = 45$ $\begin{array}{r} 29 \\ +\ 16 \\ \hline 45 \end{array}$

Yuri and Elena's team scored 45 goals altogether.

Page 7

Lesson 1.2 Finding Unknowns

To find an unknown addend in an addition problem, subtract the given numbers.

$52 + ? = 81$ → $\begin{array}{r} 81 \\ -\ 52 \\ \hline 29 \end{array}$ → $52 + 29 = 81$

Find the unknown value. Write the subtraction problem you used.

_____ + 448 = 984

$\begin{array}{r} 984 \\ -\ 448 \\ \hline 536 \end{array}$

$536 + 448 = 984$

4,251 + _____ = 9,870

$\begin{array}{r} 9870 \\ -\ 4251 \\ \hline 5,619 \end{array}$

$4,251 + 5,619 = 9,870$

Adrian had 155 marbles. Her friend Beth also had some marbles. Together, Adrian and Beth had 481 marbles. How many marbles did Beth have? How many would they have if Adrian found 5 more marbles?

$155 + ? = 481$ $\begin{array}{r} 481 \\ -\ 155 \\ \hline 326 \end{array}$ $\begin{array}{r} 481 \\ +\ 5 \\ \hline 486 \end{array}$

Beth had 326 marbles. If Adrian had 5 more marbles they would have 486 total.

Answer Key

Page 8

NAME

Lesson 1.2 Finding Unknowns

To find an unknown subtrahend in a subtraction problem, subtract the given numbers.

minuend → 175
subtrahend → − ?
difference → 38

6 15
1̶7̶5̶
− 38
137

$175 - \underline{137} = 38$

To find an unknown minuend in a subtraction problem, add the given numbers.

minuend → ?
subtrahend → − 17
difference → 115

115
+ 17
132

$132 - \underline{17} = 115$

Solve to find the unknown value.

$6,255 - \underline{} = 2,513$ $\underline{} - 329 = 171$

$6,255 - \underline{3,742} = 2,513$

$$\begin{array}{r} {}^{5\,12}6255 \\ -\ 2513 \\ \hline 3,742 \end{array}$$

$\underline{500} - 329 = 171$

$$\begin{array}{r} {}^{1}171 \\ +\ 329 \\ \hline 500 \end{array}$$

Bobbi saved some money from doing chores. He bought a computer game that cost $28. Now, Bobbi has $70 left. How much money did Bobbi have to begin with?

$? - 28 = \$70$
$70 + 28 = 98$
$\$98 - 28 = \$70$

Bobbi had $98 to begin with.

Does Bobbi have enough money left over to buy a new pair of sneakers that costs $35 and a hat that costs $27?

$\$35 + 27 = 62$
Yes, Bobbi has enough left to buy the sneakers and hat.

Page 9

NAME

Lesson 1.2 Finding Unknowns

You can use subtraction to find an unknown when adding three or more numbers.

$1 + ? + 9 + 7 = 22$

First, add the addends that are given: $1 + 9 + 7 = 17$
Then, subtract: $22 - 17 = 5$
$1 + \mathbf{5} + 9 + 7 = 22$

Solve to find the unknown value. Write the addition and subtraction sentences you used.

$\underline{} + 113 + 209 + 102 = 589$

$113 + 209 + 102 = 424$
$589 - 424 = 165$

Three friends had a picnic in the park. They each brought some fruit for dessert. One friend brought 6 bananas, one friend brought some pineapples, and one friend brought 4 apples. Altogether, the three friends had 12 pieces of fruit. How many pineapples were there?

$$\begin{array}{r} 6 \\ +\ 4 \\ \hline 10 \end{array} \qquad \begin{array}{r} 12 \\ -\ 10 \\ \hline 2 \end{array}$$

The one friend bought 2 pineapples.

If a fourth friend joins them and brings 5 peaches, how many pieces of fruit will there be altogether?

$$\begin{array}{r} 12 \\ +\ 5 \\ \hline 17 \end{array}$$

If a fourth friend comes, they will have 17 pieces of fruit.

Page 10

NAME

Lesson 1.3 Adding 3 or More Numbers

You can use a number line when adding three or more numbers.
$87 + 78 + \underline{} = 206$

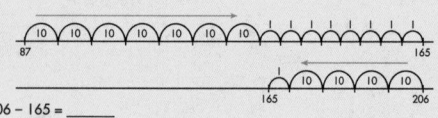

$206 - 165 = \underline{}$

$87 + 78 + \mathbf{41} = 206$

Use a number line to solve.

$315 + 173 + \underline{} + 166 = 854$ $315 + 173 + \underline{200} + 166 = 854$

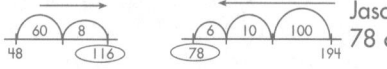

Connor, Drew, and Jason are comparing their baseball card collections. Connor has 48 cards and Drew has 68 cards. Jason also has some cards. Together, the boys have 194 baseball cards. How many does Jason have?

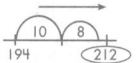

Jason has 78 cards.

Jeremy joins them. He has 18 baseball cards in his collection. How many cards do the boys have with Jeremy's collection?

With Jeremy's collection, they have 212 cards.

Page 11

NAME

Lesson 1.4 Finding Unknowns

You can write a number sentence based on a completed number line.

$138 - 71 = 67$ $67 + 71 = 138$

Write the correct addition and subtraction sentence for each number line given.

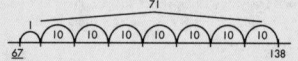

$\underline{651} - \underline{55} = \underline{596}$ $\underline{596} + \underline{55} = \underline{651}$

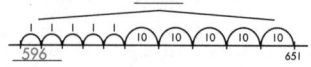

$\underline{3,475} - \underline{3,105} = \underline{370}$ $\underline{370} + \underline{3,105} = \underline{3,475}$

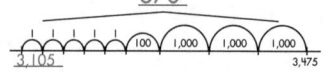

$\underline{57,291} - \underline{1,332} = \underline{55,959}$ $\underline{55,959} + \underline{1,332} = \underline{57,291}$

Answer Key

Page 12

NAME _____

Lesson 1.4 Finding Unknowns

You can use a number line to find unknown addends in an addition problem.

148 + ? = 464

Using tens and ones, count backward to the amount of the given addend.

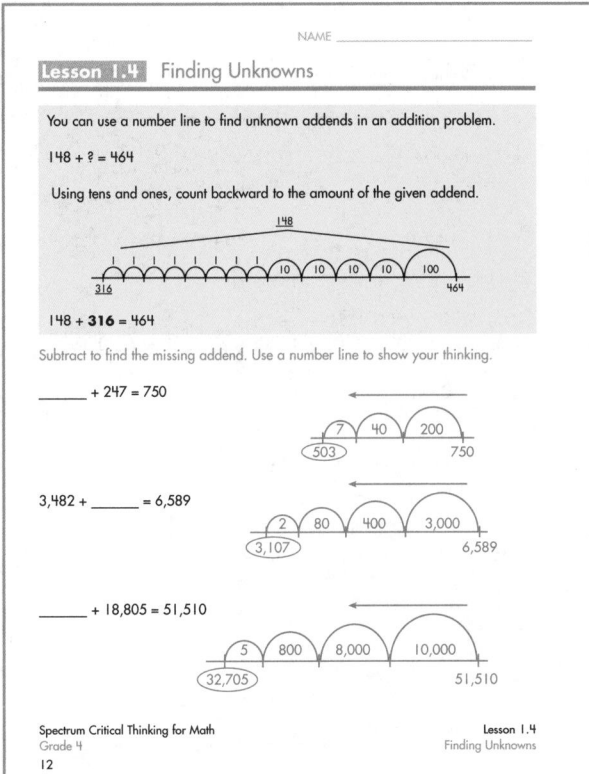

148 + **316** = 464

Subtract to find the missing addend. Use a number line to show your thinking.

_____ + 247 = 750

3,482 + _____ = 6,589

_____ + 18,805 = 51,510

Page 13

NAME _____

Lesson 1.4 Finding Unknowns

To find an unknown value in a subtraction problem, you can draw a picture.

7,198 – _____ = 5,806

Trade 1 thousand for 10 hundreds and subtract 800:

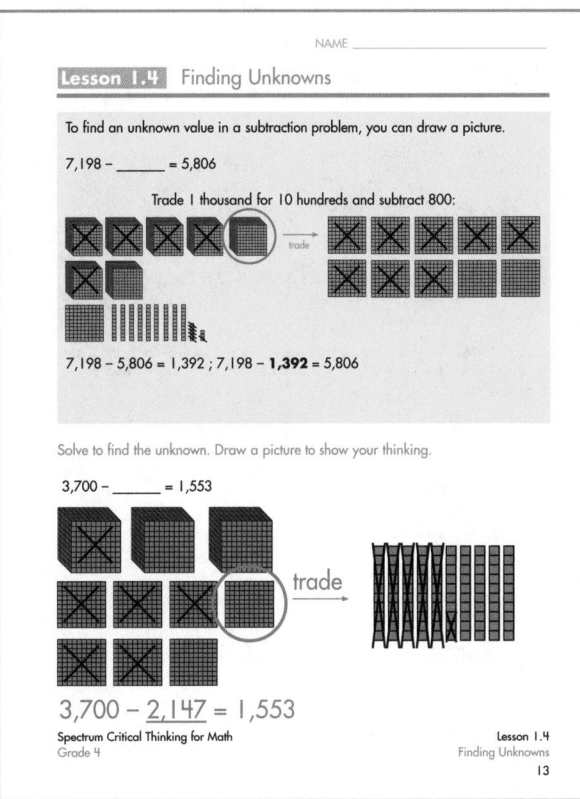

7,198 – 5,806 = 1,392 ; 7,198 – **1,392** = 5,806

Solve to find the unknown. Draw a picture to show your thinking.

3,700 – _____ = 1,553

trade

3,700 – **2,147** = 1,553

Page 14

NAME _____

Lesson 1.4 Finding Unknowns

To find an unknown value when adding numbers, you can draw a picture.

4,909 + _____ = 6,989

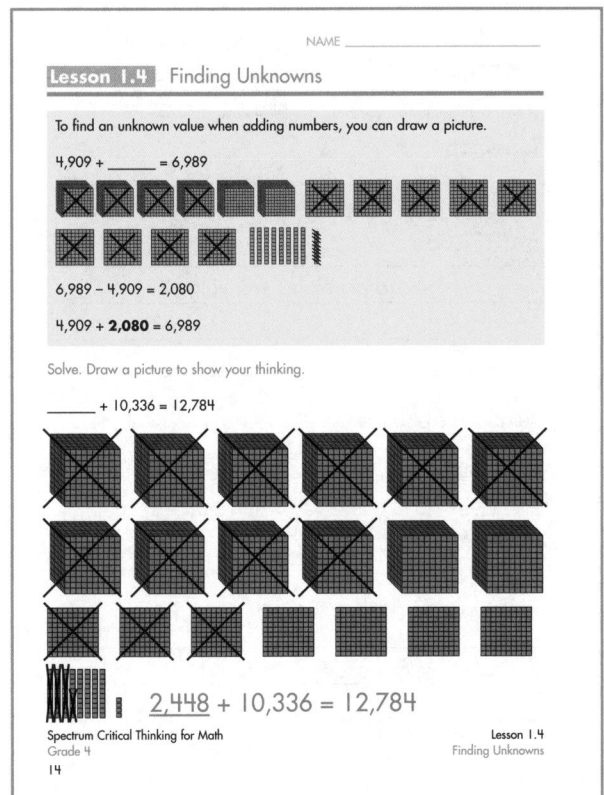

6,989 – 4,909 = 2,080

4,909 + **2,080** = 6,989

Solve. Draw a picture to show your thinking.

_____ + 10,336 = 12,784

2,448 + 10,336 = 12,784

Page 15

NAME _____

Lesson 1.4 Finding Unknowns

Solve the problems.

Draw a picture to show your work.
9,341 – _____ = 6,007

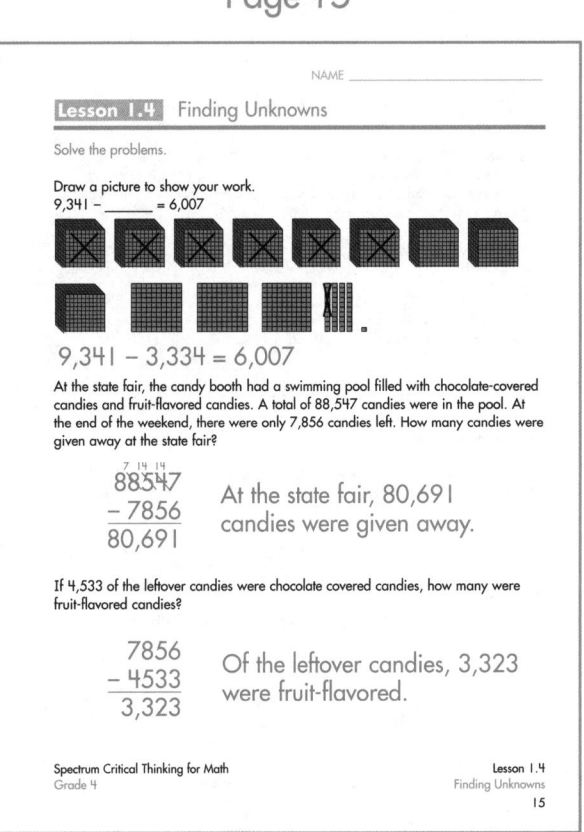

9,341 – 3,334 = 6,007

At the state fair, the candy booth had a swimming pool filled with chocolate-covered candies and fruit-flavored candies. A total of 88,547 candies were in the pool. At the end of the weekend, there were only 7,856 candies left. How many candies were given away at the state fair?

$$\begin{array}{r} {}^{7\ 14\ 14}88\cancel{5}\cancel{4}\cancel{7} \\ -\ 7856 \\ \hline 80,691 \end{array}$$

At the state fair, 80,691 candies were given away.

If 4,533 of the leftover candies were chocolate covered candies, how many were fruit-flavored candies?

$$\begin{array}{r} 7856 \\ -\ 4533 \\ \hline 3,323 \end{array}$$

Of the leftover candies, 3,323 were fruit-flavored.

Answer Key

Page 16

NAME _____

Lesson 1.4 Finding Unknowns

Solve the problems.

Draw a number line to show your work.
7,993 + _____ = 14,807

$$7,993 + 6,814 = 14,807$$

Earth is 7,926 miles wide. Saturn is much wider. The total width of Earth and Saturn is 82,926 miles. How many miles wide is Saturn? Write the number sentence you used to solve.

$$\begin{array}{r} 8\overset{7}{\cancel{8}}\overset{12}{2}926 \\ -\ 7926 \\ \hline 75,000 \end{array}$$

Saturn is 75,000 miles wide.

If you add the width of Neptune, which is 15,125 miles, how many miles wide are all 3 planets?

$$\begin{array}{r} 82926 \\ +\ 15125 \\ \hline 98,051 \end{array}$$

If you add all the widths together, it will equal 98,051 miles.

Spectrum Critical Thinking for Math
Grade 4
16

Lesson 1.4
Finding Unknowns

Page 17

NAME _____

Lesson 1.5 Adding 3 or More Multi-Digit Numbers

You can use the partition method when adding three or more numbers.

2,012 + 150 + 150 = _____

thousands	2,000 + 0 + 0	= 2,000
hundreds	0 + 100 + 100	= 200
tens	10 + 50 + 50	= 110
ones	2 + 0 + 0	= 2

2,000 + 200 + 110 + 2 = 2,312

Solve. Use the partition method to show your work.

5,009 + 4,103 + 2,705 + 1,003 = _____

thousands: 5,000 + 4,000 + 2,000 + 1,000 = 12,000
hundreds: 0 + 100 + 700 + 0 = 800
tens: 0 + 0 + 0 + 0 = 0
ones: 9 + 3 + 5 + 3 = 20

12,000 + 800 + 0 + 20 = 12,820

7,010 + 5,528 + 3,175 + 948 = _____

thousands: 7,000 + 5,000 + 3,000 + 0 = 15,000
hundreds: 0 + 500 + 100 + 900 = 1,500
tens: 10 + 20 + 70 + 40 = 140
ones: 0 + 8 + 5 + 8 = 21

15,000 + 1,500 + 140 + 21 = 16,661

Spectrum Critical Thinking for Math
Grade 4

Lesson 1.5
Adding 3 or More Multi-Digit Numbers
17

Page 18

NAME _____

Lesson 1.6 Addition and Subtraction in the Real World

Last year, 10,738 teenagers lived in Travis County. This year, 922 more teenagers moved there. How many teenagers live in Travis County now? Next month, 25 teenagers have birthdays and will no longer be teenagers. How many teenagers will live in Travis County after next month?

First, add how many teenagers lived in Travis County last year, and how many moved there this year: 10,738 + 922 = 11,660

Then, subtract the number of teenagers that have birthdays from the total number of teenagers in Travis County: 11,660 − 25 = 11,635

After next month, Travis County will have 11,635 teenagers.

Solve the problems. Show your work.

Over the weekend, the Dumon Theater sold 7,615 buckets of popcorn, 1,207 bottles of water, and 1,152 boxes of candy. How many food items did the theater sell?

$$\begin{array}{r} 7615 \\ 1207 \\ +\ 1152 \\ \hline 9,974 \end{array}$$

The theater sold 9,974 food items.

How many more buckets of popcorn than boxes of candy did the theater sell?

$$\begin{array}{r} \overset{5}{7}\overset{11}{\cancel{6}}15 \\ -\ 1152 \\ \hline 6,463 \end{array}$$

They sold 6,463 more buckets of popcorn than candy.

Spectrum Critical Thinking for Math
Grade 4
18

Lesson 1.6
Addition and Subtraction in the Real World

Page 19

NAME _____

Lesson 1.6 Addition and Subtraction in the Real World

Write a word problem to go with this addition problem. Then, solve.

10,738 + 1,327 =

$$\begin{array}{r} 10738 \\ +\ 1327 \\ \hline 12,065 \end{array}$$

Word problems will vary.

Write a word problem to go with this addition problem. Then, solve using the partition method.

1,935 + 1,690 + 130 + 117 =

thousands: 1,000 + 1,000 + 0 + 0 = 2,000
hundreds: 900 + 600 + 100 + 100 = 1,700
tens: 30 + 90 + 30 + 10 = 160
ones: 5 + 0 + 0 + 7 = 12
2,000 + 1,700 + 160 + 12 = 3,872

Word problems will vary.

Spectrum Critical Thinking for Math
Grade 4

Lesson 1.6
Addition and Subtraction in the Real World
19

Answer Key

Page 20

NAME

Lesson 1.7 Checking Answers

You can check a subtraction problem by using addition.

1,971 − 466 = 1,055
1,055 + 466 = 1,521 This answer is not correct.

Solve the problem again and recheck.

```
      6 11            1
   1,9̷7̷1̷         1,505
  −  466         + 466
   1,505          1,971  ✓ This answer is correct.
```

Use addition to check the problems. If the answer is incorrect, solve the problem again and recheck. Write the addition sentence you used to check.

512 − 167 = 287

```
   287
 + 167
   454
not correct
```

```
 4 10 12
  5̷1̷2̷
 − 167
   345
```

```
   345
 + 167
   512
 correct ✓
```

20,897 − 4,187 = 17,191

```
  17191
 + 4187
  21,378
not correct
```

```
  1 10
  2̷0̷897
 −  4187
  16,710
```

```
  16710
 + 4187
  20,897
 correct ✓
```

Spectrum Critical Thinking for Math
Grade 4
20

Lesson 1.7
Checking Answers

Page 21

NAME

Lesson 1.7 Checking Answers

You can check an addition problem by using subtraction.

14,011 + 25,126 = 40,137
40,137 − 25,126 = 15,011 This answer is incorrect.

Solve the problem again and recheck.

```
   14,011        39,137
 + 25,126      − 25,126
   39,137        14,011  ✓ This answer is correct.
```

Use subtraction to check the problems. If the answer is incorrect, solve the problem again and recheck. Write the addition sentence you used to check.

43,106 + 19,847 = 75,103

```
 6 14 10 9 13
  7̷5̷1̷0̷3̷
 − 19847
  55,256
not correct
```

```
  43106
 + 19847
  62,953
```

```
 5 12   4 13
  6̷2̷9̷5̷3̷
 − 19847
  43,106
 correct ✓
```

1,599 + 3,100 = 4,998

```
   4998
 − 3100
  1,898
not correct
```

```
  1599
 + 3100
  4,699
```

```
  4699
 − 3100
  1,599
 correct ✓
```

Spectrum Critical Thinking for Math
Grade 4
21

Lesson 1.7
Checking Answers

Page 22

NAME

💡 **Check What You Learned**

Adding and Subtracting through 5 Digits

Read the problem carefully and solve. Show your work under each question.

Four Boy Scout troops collected canned goods to donate to the Rossville food bank. At the end of the week, Troop 151 had 92 cans. Troop 152 had 213 cans. Troop 153 had 88 cans and Troop 154 had 105 cans.

1. How many more cans did Troop 152 and 154 collect than Troop 151 and 153? Show your work using a number line.

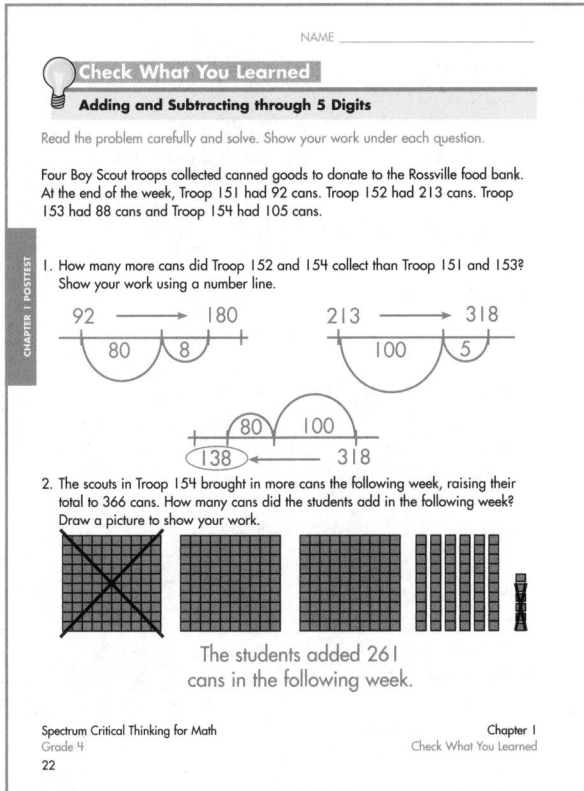

2. The scouts in Troop 154 brought in more cans the following week, raising their total to 366 cans. How many cans did the students add in the following week? Draw a picture to show your work.

The students added 261 cans in the following week.

Spectrum Critical Thinking for Math
Grade 4
22

Chapter 1
Check What You Learned

Page 23

NAME

💡 **Check What You Learned**

Adding and Subtracting through 5 Digits

Read the problem carefully and solve. Show your work under each question.

The Penny Club at Avery Elementary School collects pennies and donates them to a local charity every fall and spring. There are 4 members of the club: Kelly, Oliver, Pablo, and Reese. The following chart shows how many pennies each member collected last fall and spring.

Member	Fall	Spring
Kelly	5,899	16,522
Oliver	45,784	13,524
Pablo	9,632	85,211
Reese	963	48,599

3. How many more pennies did the club donate in the spring than in the fall? Use the traditional methods to show your work.

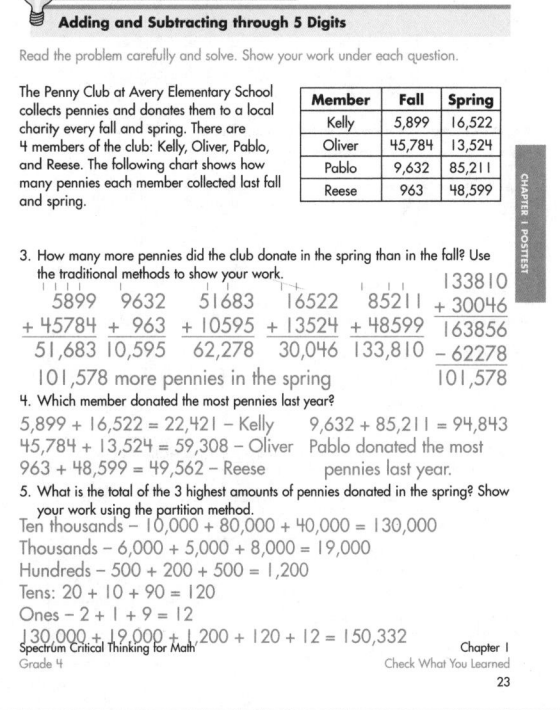

```
   5899     9632    51683    16522    85211
 + 45784   + 963  + 10595  + 13524  + 48599
  51,683  10,595   62,278   30,046  133,810
```

```
  133810
 + 30046
  163856
 − 62278
  101,578
```

101,578 more pennies in the spring

4. Which member donated the most pennies last year?

5,899 + 16,522 = 22,421 – Kelly   9,632 + 85,211 = 94,843
45,784 + 13,524 = 59,308 – Oliver   Pablo donated the most
963 + 48,599 = 49,562 – Reese   pennies last year.

5. What is the total of the 3 highest amounts of pennies donated in the spring? Show your work using the partition method.

Ten thousands – 10,000 + 80,000 + 40,000 = 130,000
Thousands – 6,000 + 5,000 + 8,000 = 19,000
Hundreds – 500 + 200 + 500 = 1,200
Tens: 20 + 10 + 90 = 120
Ones – 2 + 1 + 9 = 12
130,000 + 19,000 + 1,200 + 120 + 12 = 150,332

Spectrum Critical Thinking for Math
Grade 4
23

Chapter 1
Check What You Learned

Answer Key

Page 24

NAME _____

Check What You Know

Numeration

Andrew is thinking of a number. The number has a 3 in the tens place. The number in the ones place is three more than 5. There is a 6 in the ten thousands place. The number in the hundreds place is between 0 and 2. The number in the thousands place is 5 less than 10.

Fill in the blanks for Andrew's number.

1. Number name: <u>sixty-five thousand one hundred thirty-eight</u>

2. Expanded form <u>(6x10,000) + (5x1,000) + (1x100) + (3x10) + (8x1)</u>

3. Round the number to the nearest thousand: <u>65,000</u>

Jonathan is thinking of a number. This number has a 9 in the thousands place as well as in the 2 places to the right. The number in the ones place is double the number in the ten thousands place. The number in the hundred thousands place is 6. The number in the ten thousands place is 4 less than 6. The number in the millions place is between 4 and 6.

Fill in the blanks for Jonathan's number.

4. Number Name: <u>five million six hundred twenty-nine thousand nine hundred ninety-four</u>

5. Expanded Form: <u>(5x1,000,000) (6x100,000) + (2x10,000) + (9x1,000) + (9x100) + (9x10) + (4x1)</u>

6. Round the number to the nearest hundred thousand: <u>5,600,000</u>

7. Compare Andrew and Jonathan's numbers using <, >, or =.

<u>5,629,994</u> <u>></u> <u>65,138</u>

Spectrum Critical Thinking for Math
Grade 4
24

Chapter 2
Check What You Know

Page 25

NAME _____

Lesson 2.1 Place Value

Numbers are made up of the digits 0–9 in different places. The place value of whole numbers goes from right to left. The chart below shows the place value of each digit in the number 1,359,264.

Place Value	1,000,000 Millions	100,000 Hundred Thousands	10,000 Ten Thousands	1,000 Thousands	100 Hundreds	10 Tens	1 Ones
Digit Value	1,000,000	300,000	50,000	9,000	200	60	4

Answer the questions.

Isabella is thinking of a number in the hundred thousands. The first digit is equal to the number of digits in the number. The number has 20 tens and twice as many thousands. The number of ones is an odd number that is less than 5 and greater than the digit in the hundreds place. What is Isabella's number?

<u>6</u>   <u>4</u>   <u>0</u>,   <u>2</u>   <u>0</u>   <u>3</u>

Using the digits 7, 8, 5, 9 and 2, write three numbers: the smallest number possible, the largest number possible, and a number between the largest and smallest numbers.

smallest — <u>2 5, 7 8 9</u>

middle — <u>7 8, 5 9 2</u>

largest — <u>9 8, 7 5 2</u>

(this will vary, check for accuracy)

Spectrum Critical Thinking for Math
Grade 4

Lesson 2.1
Place Value
25

Page 26

NAME _____

Lesson 2.2 Writing Numbers

There are 3 ways to write numbers:

Standard form Using numerals, place a comma every 3 digits going from right to left: 25,845

Number name Using words, include each digit as well as its place value: twenty five thousand eight hundred forty five

Expanded form Shows how each digit is multiplied by its place value: (2 x 10,000) + (5 x 1,000) + (8 x 100) + (4 x 10) + (5 x 1)

Write the missing forms of each number.

standard form	78,985
number name	seventy-eight thousand nine hundred eighty-five
expanded form	(7x10,000) + (8x1,000) + (9x100) + (8x10) + (5x1)

standard form	276,430
number name	two hundred seventy-six thousand four hundred thirty
expanded form	(2x100,000) + (7x10,000) + (6x1,000) + (4x100) + (3x10)

standard form	4,304
number name	four thousand three hundred four
expanded form	(4 x1,000) + (3 x 100) + (4 x1)

Spectrum Critical Thinking for Math
Grade 4
26

Lesson 2.2
Writing Numbers

Page 27

NAME _____

Lesson 2.3 Rounding

To round 56,348 to the nearest thousand, follow these steps.
1. Find the digit in the thousands place: 5<u>6</u>,348.
2. Look right. The digit in the hundreds place will decide if the digit in the thousands place gets rounded up to 7 or stays the same at 6.
3. The digit in the hundreds place is 3. Since 3 is less than 5, the digit in the thousands place, 6, stays the same.
4. All digits to the right of the thousands place become zeros.
5. 56,348 rounded to the nearest thousand is 56,000.

Round each number to all of the nearest place values.

187,349

tens: <u>187,350</u>
hundreds: <u>187,300</u>
thousands: <u>187,000</u>
ten thousands: <u>190,000</u>
hundred thousands: <u>200,000</u>

58,045

tens: <u>58,050</u>
hundreds: <u>58,000</u>
thousands: <u>58,000</u>
ten thousands: <u>60,000</u>
hundred thousands: <u>100,000</u>

567,503

tens: <u>567,500</u>
hundreds: <u>567,500</u>
thousands: <u>568,000</u>
ten thousands: <u>570,000</u>
hundred thousands: <u>600,000</u>

285,393

tens: <u>285,390</u>
hundreds: <u>285,400</u>
thousands: <u>285,000</u>
ten thousands: <u>290,000</u>
hundred thousands: <u>300,000</u>

Spectrum Critical Thinking for Math
Grade 4

Lesson 2.3
Rounding
27

Answer Key

Page 28

NAME _____

Lesson 2.3 Rounding

Read each problem carefully. Round the numbers given to the nearest place value given.

Callista is writing a report about the recent election for the district attorney of her state. The chart below shows how many votes each candidate received.

Candidate	Votes
Mrs. Benson	2,431,584
Mr. Ling	547,965
Ms. Shaw	249,632

Callista wants to round the number of votes Mrs. Benson received. What is this number rounded to the nearest million?

$$2,431,584 \longrightarrow 2,000,000$$

What is the number of votes Ms. Shaw received rounded to the nearest ten thousand?

$$249,632 \longrightarrow 250,000$$

Callista rounds the number of votes Mr. Ling received to the nearest hundred thousand. What does she get for an answer?

$$547,965 \longrightarrow 500,000$$

To determine how many people voted in the election, Callista rounds each candidate's total votes to the nearest hundred thousand and added them together. What does she get for an answer?

```
  2400000
   200000
+  500000
  3,100,000
```

About 3,100,000 people voted for any of the 3 candidates.

Page 29

NAME _____

Lesson 2.4 Comparing Numbers

To compare the numbers 12,317 and 12,713, line them up as shown below. This shows you which digits have the same place value.

ten thousands	thousands	hundreds	tens	ones
1	2	3	1	7
1	2	7	1	3

Begin with the digit farthest to the left. Both numbers have 1 in the ten thousands place and 2 in the thousands place. The digits in the hundreds place (3 and 7) are different, so use them to determine which number is greater.

The symbols > (greater than), < (less than), and = (equal to) are used to compare numbers.

12,713 > 12,317   OR   12,317 < 12,713

Order the set of numbers from **least** to **greatest**.

5,635,042   5,653,024   5,536,204   6,536,042

$$5,536,204; \ 5,635,042; \ 5,653,024; \ 6,536,042$$

Four friends each had a coin collection. Darius had 45,673 coins in his collection. Forrest had 46,537 coins in his collection. Evan had 45,637 coins in his collection, and Jaime had 44,657 coins in his collection. Order the friends' coin collections from **greatest** to **least**.

$$46,537; \ 45,673; \ 45,637; \ 44,657$$

Page 30

NAME _____

Lesson 2.4 Comparing Numbers

Noah and Molly are playing a math game called Number Spin. They spin a spinner labeled 1 – 9 and use each number they spin to make larger numbers. They change the number of digits in the numbers they create each round. The chart below shows the numbers they made each round.

Round	Noah	Molly
1	5,965	5,874
2	2,631,891	2,555,873
3	94,321	84,110
4	544,331	975,211

Write <, >, or = to compare Noah and Molly's numbers from round one.

5,965 > 5,874

Molly wants to compare the numbers in round three. What should she write to compare them?

$$94,321 > 84,110$$

Who made the larger number in round four? Compare the 2 numbers using <, >, or =.

Molly made the larger number in round 4.
$$975,211 > 544,331$$

Page 31

NAME _____

Check What You Learned

Numeration

Write the smallest and the largest number you can make with each set of digits.

7, 5, 2, 8, 4

1. Largest: 87,542
2. Smallest: 24,578

6, 3, 1, 7, 9

3. Largest: 97,631
4. Smallest: 13,679

Compare the two largest numbers and two smallest numbers above using <, >, or =.

5. Largest Numbers

87,542 < 97,631

6. Smallest Numbers

24,578 > 13,679

7. Write the largest of the four numbers in expanded form:

(9×10,000) + (7×1,000) + (6×100) + (3×10) + 1

8. Write the smallest of the four numbers as a number name:

thirteen thousand six hundred seventy-nine

9. Round the largest number to the nearest ten thousand. 100,000

10. Round the smallest number to the nearest thousand. 14,000

CHAPTER 2 POSTTEST

Answer Key

Page 32

NAME

Check What You Know

Multiplication and Division

Read carefully and solve. Show your work under each question.

Tiffany places an order for office supplies. She orders 18 boxes of blue pens. There are 45 pens in each box. Paperclips come in boxes of 1,543, and she orders 6 boxes. She orders 12 boxes of rulers, and 105 come in each box.

1. How many total paperclips does Tiffany order? Show your work using the traditional method.

$$\begin{array}{r} 18 \\ \times\ 45 \\ \hline 90 \\ +\ 72 \\ \hline 810 \end{array}$$

810 blue pens

2. How many rulers does Tiffany order? Show your work using the grid method.

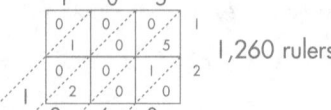

1,260 rulers

3. When Tiffany receives the order, she finds that 7 of the 18 boxes are filled with red pens instead of blue pens. How many blue pens does Tiffany have from this order?

$$\begin{array}{r} 18 \\ -\ 7 \\ \hline 11 \end{array}$$

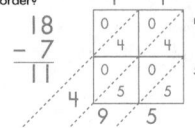

She has 495 blue pens from this order.

Spectrum Critical Thinking for Math
Grade 4
32

Chapter 3
Check What You Know

Page 33

NAME

Check What You Know

Multiplication and Division

Read carefully and solve. Show your work under each question.

Walsh's Hardware is having a big sale. The staff workers are gathering tools and other items into groups for the sale.

4. Benjamin's boss gives him 4,304 bolts. His boss says to put them in bags of 8 bolts each. How many full bags of bolts will he have? Will he have any left over? If so, how many? Show your work using the partial quotients method.

$$\begin{array}{r} 538 \\ 8)\overline{4304} \\ 4000 \quad 500 \\ \hline 304 \\ 240 \quad 30 \\ \hline 64 \\ -\ 64 \quad 8 \\ \hline 0 \end{array}$$

He will have 538 full bags of bolts. He will not have any left over.

5. Brooke has 732 screwdrivers. She puts them in sets of 5. How many screwdrivers will be left over when she is finished? Show your work using long division.

$$\begin{array}{r} 146\ r2 \\ 5)\overline{732} \\ -\ 5 \\ \hline 23 \\ -\ 20 \\ \hline 32 \\ -\ 30 \\ \hline 2 \end{array}$$

146 r2

There will be 2 screwdrivers left over when she is finished.

6. The sale items are worth $8,958 in all. The sale will last for 3 days. How much money will the store make per day if the sales are equal each day? Show your work using short division.

$$\begin{array}{r} 2,986 \\ 3)\overline{8958} \end{array}$$

$2,986 per day

Spectrum Critical Thinking for Math
Grade 4
33

Chapter 3
Check What You Know

Page 34

NAME

Lesson 3.1 Prime and Composite Numbers

A number is called prime if its only factors are 1 and itself. For example, 7 is a prime number. The only factors of 7 are 1 and 7.

A number is called composite if it has more than two factors. For example, 8 is a composite number. 1, 2, 4, and 8 are all factors of 8.

A factor tree is a tool that breaks a number down into its prime factors.

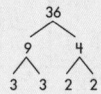

List the factors of each number. Then, label each number as prime or composite.

Number	Factors	Prime or Composite?
7	1,7	prime
18	1,2,3,6,9,18	composite
29	1,29	prime

Write 2 composite numbers and create factor trees for each.

Answers will vary. Possible answers:

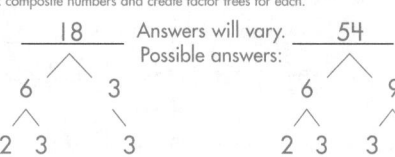

Spectrum Critical Thinking for Math
Grade 4
34

Lesson 3.1
Prime and Composite Numbers

Page 35

NAME

Lesson 3.2 Multiplication: Traditional Method

$$\begin{array}{r} 72 \\ \times\ 8 \\ \hline 6 \end{array}$$
Multiply 2 ones by 8.
$2 \times 8 = 16$ or $10 + 6$
Put 6 under the ones place.
Add the 10 above the 7.

$$\begin{array}{r} 72 \\ \times\ 8 \\ \hline 576 \end{array}$$
Multiply 7 tens by 8.
Then, add 1 ten.
$70 \times 8 = 560 \rightarrow 560 + 10$
$= 570$ or $500 + 70$

Answer the questions. Show your work.

There are 38 chicken farms near a New York town. Each farm has 7 barns and in each barn are 78 chickens. How many chickens are on each farm?

$$\begin{array}{r} 78 \\ \times\ 7 \\ \hline 546 \end{array}$$
chickens
barns
total chickens on each farm

How many total barns are there?

$$\begin{array}{r} 38 \\ \times\ 7 \\ \hline 266 \end{array}$$
farms
barns
total barns

Spectrum Critical Thinking for Math
Grade 4
35

Lesson 3.2
Multiplication: Traditional Method

Answer Key

Page 36

NAME _____

Lesson 3.2 Multiplication: Grid Method

$704 \times \underline{8} =$ _____

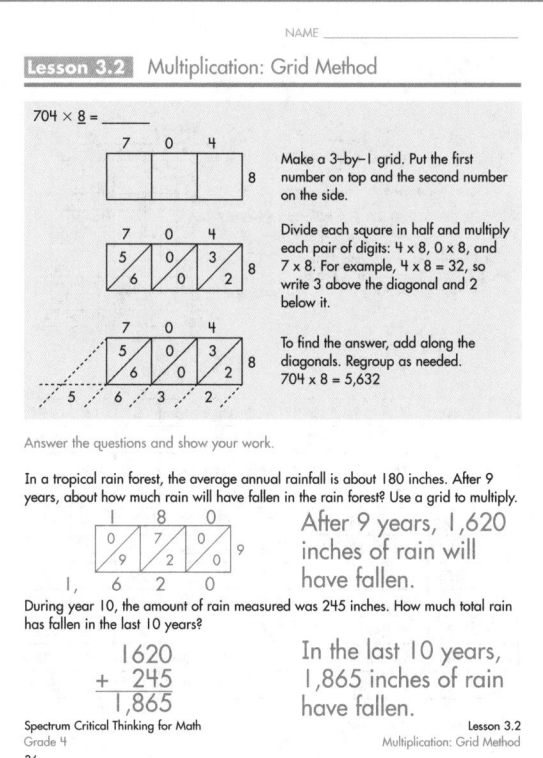

Make a 3-by-1 grid. Put the first number on top and the second number on the side.

Divide each square in half and multiply each pair of digits: 4 x 8, 0 x 8, and 7 x 8. For example, 4 x 8 = 32, so write 3 above the diagonal and 2 below it.

To find the answer, add along the diagonals. Regroup as needed. 704 x 8 = 5,632

Answer the questions and show your work.

In a tropical rain forest, the average annual rainfall is about 180 inches. After 9 years, about how much rain will have fallen in the rain forest? Use a grid to multiply.

After 9 years, 1,620 inches of rain will have fallen.

During year 10, the amount of rain measured was 245 inches. How much total rain has fallen in the last 10 years?

$$1620 + 245 = 1,865$$

In the last 10 years, 1,865 inches of rain have fallen.

Page 37

NAME _____

Lesson 3.3 Multiplication: Repeated Addition

You can multiply using the repeated addition method.

$3,421 \times 3 =$ _____

$$\begin{array}{r} 3,421 \\ 3,421 \\ + 3,421 \\ \hline 10,263 \end{array}$$

Answer the questions using repeated addition. Show your work.

A school of 1,786 students went on a field trip to collect sand dollars. If the students collected 4 sand dollars each, how many sand dollars did they collect?

$$\begin{array}{r} {\scriptstyle 3\,3\,2} \\ 1786 \\ 1786 \\ 1786 \\ + 1786 \\ \hline 7,144 \end{array}$$

They collected 7,144 sand dollars.

A different school of 2,641 students also went on a field trip and collected seashells. If each student from that school collected 5 seashells each, how many total sand dollars and seashells did the schools collect?

$$\begin{array}{r} {\scriptstyle 3\,2} \\ 2641 \\ 2641 \\ 2641 \\ 2641 \\ + 2641 \\ \hline 13,205 \end{array} \qquad \begin{array}{r} {\scriptstyle 1} \\ 13205 \\ + 7144 \\ \hline 20,349 \end{array}$$

The schools collected 20,349 total sand dollars and seashells.

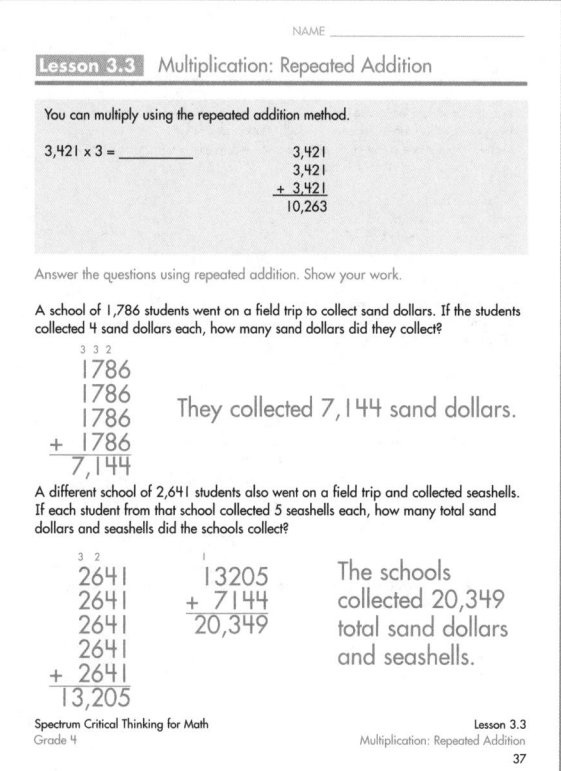

Page 38

NAME _____

Lesson 3.4 Multiplication Tables

To complete a multiplication table, multiply all the numbers in the **In** column by the same number to get the answer in the **Out** column.

Rule: Multiply by 3

In	Out
3	9
4	12
5	15

Complete each table.

Rule: Multiply by 19

In	Out
1	19
3	57
6	114
9	171

Rule: Multiply by 1,526

In	Out
2	3,052
3	4,578
4	6,104
5	7,630

Rule: Multiply by 7 and add 12.

In	Out
515	3,617
894	6,270
202	1,426
485	3,407

Page 39

NAME _____

Lesson 3.5 Multiplication

Write a word problem to go with this multiplication problem. Solve using the traditional multiplication method.

$71 \times 67 = 4,757$

$$\begin{array}{r} 71 \\ \times\ 67 \\ \hline 497 \\ +426 \\ \hline 4,757 \end{array}$$

Word problems will vary.

Solve this problem using the grid method. Show your work.

$841 \times 71 =$

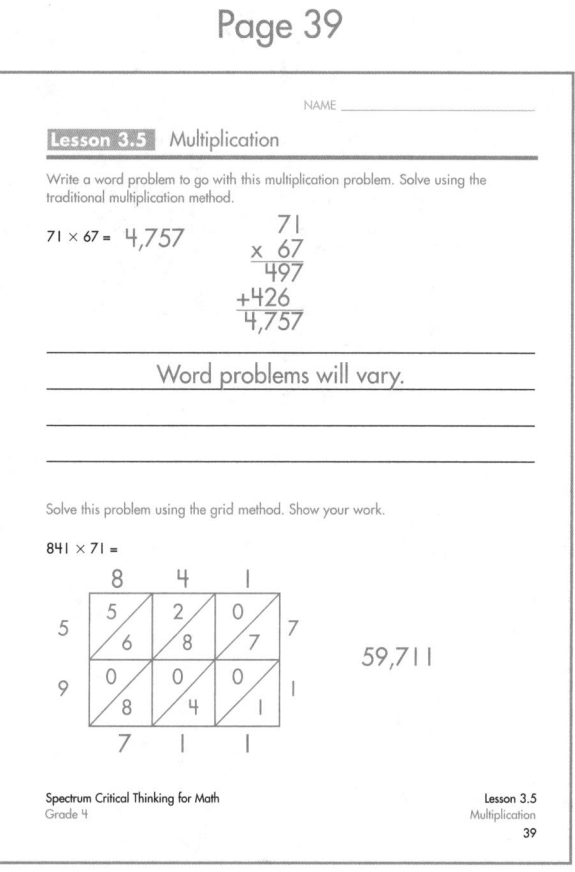

59,711

Answer Key

Page 40

Lesson 3.6 Multiplication in the Real World

A cable program loans channel boxes to 19 community centers for a trial program. If there are 13 boxes for each center, how many boxes are being loaned? Four more community centers would like to join the program. How many more channel boxes will be needed?

To answer the first question, multiply 19 community centers by 13 channel boxes. 247 boxes are being loaned.

$$\begin{array}{r} 2 \\ 19 \\ \times\ 13 \\ \hline 57 \\ +\ 190 \\ \hline 247 \end{array} \Big\} add$$

To answer the second question, multiply 13 channel boxes by 4 community centers. 52 more boxes will be needed.

$$\begin{array}{r} 1 \\ 13 \\ \times\ 4 \\ \hline 52 \end{array}$$

Solve the problems. Show your work.

Orlando's Orchards grows 2 types of apples. One is red and the other is green. The trees that grow red apples are planted in 24 rows with 72 trees in each row. How many of the trees in the orchard grow red apples?

$$\begin{array}{r} 2 \\ 24 \\ \times\ 72 \\ \hline 48 \\ 1680 \\ \hline 1,728 \end{array}$$

There are 1,728 trees in the orchard that grow red apples.

The trees that grow green apples are planted in 22 rows with 38 trees in each row. Next season, the orchard will add 3 more green apple trees to each row of green apple trees. How many total green apple trees will there be next season?

$$\begin{array}{r} 1 \\ 22 \\ \times\ 38 \\ \hline 176 \\ 660 \\ \hline 836 \end{array} \quad \begin{array}{r} 22 \\ \times\ 3 \\ \hline 66 \end{array} \quad \begin{array}{r} 11 \\ 836 \\ +\ 66 \\ \hline 902 \end{array}$$

Next season, there will be 902 green apple trees.

Page 41

Lesson 3.7 Division Facts

$$\text{divisor} \longrightarrow 5\overline{)45} \longleftarrow \text{quotient / dividend}$$

To check your answer, do the inverse operation.
If $45 \div 5 = 9$, then $5 \times 9 = 45$ must be true.

Using the division table, find 45 in the 5 column. The quotient is named at the beginning of the row.

5-column → (divisors)

x	0	1	2	3	4	5	6	7	8	9
0	0	0	0	0	0	0	0	0	0	0
1	0	1	2	3	4	5	6	7	8	9
2	0	2	4	6	8	10	12	14	16	18
3	0	3	6	9	12	15	18	21	24	27
4	0	4	8	12	16	20	24	28	32	36
5	0	5	10	15	20	25	30	35	40	45
6	0	6	12	18	24	30	36	42	48	54
7	0	7	14	21	28	35	42	49	56	63
8	0	8	16	24	32	40	48	56	64	72
9	0	9	18	27	36	45	54	63	72	81

(quotients) / quotient

Complete the table below.

X	10	11	12	13	14	15	16	17	18	19
10	100	110	120	130	140	150	160	170	180	190
11	110	121	132	143	154	165	176	187	198	209
12	120	132	144	156	168	180	192	204	216	228
13	130	143	156	169	182	195	208	221	234	247
14	140	154	168	182	196	210	224	238	252	266
15	150	165	180	195	210	225	240	255	270	285
16	160	176	192	208	224	240	256	272	288	304
17	170	187	204	221	238	255	272	289	306	323
18	180	198	216	234	252	270	288	306	324	342
19	190	209	228	247	266	285	304	323	342	361

Page 42

Lesson 3.8 Division: Long Division Method

8×4

$$\begin{array}{r} 4 \\ 8\overline{)33} \\ -32 \\ \hline 1 \end{array}$$

33 is between 32 and 40, so $33 \div 8$ is between 4 and 5. The ones digit is 4.

x	1	2	3	4	5
8	8	16	24	32	40

Since $33 - 32 = 1$ and 1 is less than 8, the remainder 1 is recorded like this.

$$\begin{array}{r} 4\ r\ 1 \\ 8\overline{)33} \\ -32 \\ \hline 1 \end{array}$$

Divide using long division. Show your work.

7)8,921   3)843

$$\begin{array}{r} 1,274\ r3 \\ 7\overline{)8921} \\ -7 \\ \hline 19 \\ -14 \\ \hline 52 \\ -49 \\ \hline 31 \\ -28 \\ \hline 3 \end{array} \qquad \begin{array}{r} 281 \\ 3\overline{)843} \\ -6 \\ \hline 24 \\ -24 \\ \hline 0 \end{array}$$

Page 43

Lesson 3.9 Division in the Real World

Two basketball teams carpool to their game. There are 23 players on Amanda's team. Each car for Amanda's team can hold 4 players. There are 22 players on Ben's team. Each car for Ben's team can hold 5 players. Ben's team has 4 cars.

How many cars can Amanda's team fill? How many players will be left over?

$$\begin{array}{r} 5\ r3 \\ 4\overline{)23} \\ -20 \\ \hline 3 \end{array}$$

Amanda's team will fill 5 cars and have 3 players left over.

How many cars will Amanda's team need to take all the players to the game? Explain your answer.

Amanda's team will need to take 6 cars so the 3 players can also get to the game.

Does Ben's team have enough cars to take all their players to the game? If not, how many players still need a ride?

$$\begin{array}{r} 4\ r2 \\ 5\overline{)22} \\ -20 \\ \hline 2 \end{array}$$

Ben's team does not have enough cars because 2 more people need to ride.

Page 44

NAME _____

Lesson 3.10 Division: Partial Quotients Method

The partial quotients method uses estimation to solve division problems.

First, draw a line down the right side of the problem.
Think of easy numbers to decide how many 7s can go into 87. Ten is an easy number.

You have 17 left. Again, think of an easy number to decide how many 7s can go into 17. Two 7s is 14.

You have 3 left. Three is less than 7, so you are done dividing.
Now, add the numbers you estimated on the right side.
Your answer is 12 with a remainder of 3.

$$\begin{array}{r} 12\ r3 \\ 7\overline{)87} \\ -70 \quad 10 \\ \hline 17 \\ -14 \quad 2 \\ \hline 3 \end{array}$$

less than → add → remainder

Divide using the partial quotients method. Show your work.

A service club went out to pick up litter in the park. They collected 558 bags of litter. If each member collected the same amount, how many bags did all 5 members collect? How many extra bags were collected?

$$\begin{array}{r} 111\ r3 \\ 5\overline{)558} \\ -500 \quad 100 \\ \hline 58 \\ -50 \quad 10 \\ \hline 8 \\ -5 \quad 1 \\ \hline 3 \end{array}$$

Each member collected 111 bags. A total of 3 extra bags were collected.

Page 45

NAME _____

Lesson 3.11 Division: Short Division Method

Short division is similar to long division, except that you complete the multiplication and subtraction in your head.

$$\begin{array}{r} 788\ r2 \\ 5\overline{)39^{4}4^{2}2} \end{array}$$

5 goes into 39 7 times. Write 7 on the line.
7 x 5 = 35. Mentally subtract: 39 − 35 = 4.

Write a small 4 between the 9 and the 4 to create 44. 5 goes into 44 8 times. Write 8 on the line.
5 x 8 = 40. Mentally subtract: 44 − 40 = 4.

Write a small 4 between the 4 and the 2 to create 42. 5 goes into 42 8 times. Write 8 on the line.

5 x 8 = 40. Mentally subtract: 42 − 40 = 2. This is the remainder. Your answer is 788 r2.

The school supply store received a shipment of 7,295 pens. If the pens are packed in 5 boxes, how many pens are in each box?

$$\begin{array}{r} 1,459 \\ 5\overline{)7^{2}2^{2}9^{4}5} \end{array}$$

1,459 pens are in each box.

The store is supposed to receive 3 more boxes of pens tomorrow with the same number in each box. How many pens will the school supply store receive tomorrow?

$$\begin{array}{r} {\scriptstyle 1\ 1\ 2} \\ 1459 \\ \times \quad 3 \\ \hline 4,377 \end{array}$$

The store will receive 4,377 pens tomorrow.

Page 46

NAME _____

Lesson 3.12 Division

Write a word problem to go with this division problem. Solve using short division.

$$9\overline{)3466}$$

$$\begin{array}{r} 385\ r1 \\ 9\overline{)3^{4}4^{7}6^{4}6} \end{array}$$

385 r1

_____

Word problems will vary.

_____

_____

Solve this problem using the partial quotients method. Show your work.

$$7\overline{)4986}$$

$$\begin{array}{r} 712\ r2 \\ 7\overline{)4986} \\ -4900 \quad 700 \\ \hline 86 \\ -70 \quad 10 \\ \hline 16 \\ -14 \quad 2 \\ \hline 2 \end{array}$$

Page 47

NAME _____

Lesson 3.13 Division in the Real World

Read the problem carefully and solve. Show your work under each question.

A textbook store is packing boxes full of books to ship. Each box can only hold one type of book. Each type of book must be divided evenly between each box. There are 148 mathematics textbooks and 78 literature textbooks. There are 40 music textbooks and 206 business textbooks.

If the literature textbooks are packed in 6 boxes, how many will be in each box?

13 textbooks will be in each box w/ none left over.

$$\begin{array}{r} 13 \\ 6\overline{)78} \\ -6 \downarrow \\ \hline 18 \\ -18 \\ \hline 0 \end{array}$$

The bookstore plans to use 9 boxes to ship the business textbooks. How many will fit in each box? How many will be left over?

22 business textbooks will fit in each box w/8 left over.

$$\begin{array}{r} 22\ r8 \\ 9\overline{)206} \\ -18 \downarrow \\ \hline 26 \\ -18 \\ \hline 8 \end{array}$$

If 5 music textbooks can fit into each box, how many boxes will the store need to ship all of them?

They can fill 8 boxes with music text books.

$$\begin{array}{r} 8 \\ 5\overline{)40} \\ -40 \\ \hline 0 \end{array}$$

The store only has 4 boxes left to ship all of the mathematics textbooks. Will all the books fit or will there be some left over?

Yes, all the math books will fit into 4 boxes.

$$\begin{array}{r} 37 \\ 4\overline{)148} \\ -12 \downarrow \\ \hline 28 \\ -28 \\ \hline 0 \end{array}$$

Answer Key

Page 48

Lesson 3.14 Multiplication: Dividing to Find Unknowns

To find an unknown number in a multiplication problem, divide the two numbers you are given.

$$\begin{array}{r} 5 \\ \times \boxed{} \\ \hline 45 \end{array} \qquad \begin{array}{r} 9 \\ 5)\overline{45} \\ \\ \hline 0 \end{array} \qquad \begin{array}{r} \boxed{} \\ \times \quad 2 \\ \hline 1,870 \end{array} \qquad \begin{array}{r} 935 \\ 2)\overline{1870} \\ -18\downarrow \\ \hline 07 \\ -6\downarrow \\ \hline 10 \\ -10 \\ \hline 0 \end{array}$$

Find each unknown number by dividing. Write the division problem you used.

$$\begin{array}{r} \boxed{2,818} \\ \times \quad 3 \\ \hline 8,454 \end{array} \qquad \begin{array}{r} 2818 \\ 3)\overline{8,454} \\ -6\downarrow \\ \hline 24 \\ -24\downarrow \\ \hline 05 \\ -3\downarrow \\ \hline 24 \\ \end{array} \qquad \begin{array}{r} \boxed{36} \\ \times \quad 4 \\ \hline 144 \end{array} \qquad \begin{array}{r} 36 \\ 4)\overline{144} \\ -12\downarrow \\ \hline 24 \\ -24 \\ \hline 0 \end{array}$$

Tyler had 3 boxes of matchbox cars in his toy room. His little sister dumped all of the boxes out onto the floor. There were 534 cars on the toy room floor. Tyler wants to put the cars back into the boxes. Each box held an equal amount of cars. How many toy cars were in each box?

$$\begin{array}{r} 178 \\ 3)\overline{534} \\ -3\downarrow \\ \hline 23 \\ -21\downarrow \\ \hline 24 \\ -24 \\ \hline 0 \end{array}$$

There were 178 toy cars in each box.

Page 49

Check What You Learned

Multiplication and Division

Read carefully and solve. Show your work under each question.

Students at two schools are having a contest to collect soda cans and bottles for a charity drive.

1. Banksville has 643 students. Each student collects 31 cans during the contest. How many cans do the students collect altogether? Use the traditional method to multiply.

$$\begin{array}{r} 643 \\ \times \quad 31 \\ \hline 643 \\ + 19,290 \\ \end{array}$$

The students collected 19,933 cans altogether.

2. Oaktown has 189 students. Each student collects 9 bottles. How many bottles do they collect in total? Use the grid method to multiply.

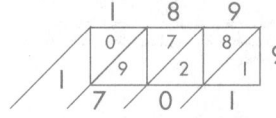

The students 9 collect 1,701 bottles in total.

3. The contest lasts 18 weeks. One student, Armando, collects 28 cans per week. How many cans does Armando collect during the contest? Use the traditional method to multiply.

$$\begin{array}{r} 26 \\ \times \quad 18 \\ \hline 208 \\ + 260 \\ \hline 468 \end{array} \text{ cans}$$

Page 50

Check What You Learned

Multiplication and Division

Solve each problem. Show your work under each question.

4. A diner has 195 seats, with 5 seats at each table. How many tables does the diner have? Use the partial quotients method to divide.

$$\begin{array}{r} 39 \\ 5)\overline{195} \\ -15\downarrow \\ \hline 45 \\ 45 \\ \hline 0 \end{array}$$

The diner has 39 tables.

5. Dion buys 4 comic books every week. If Dion has 208 comic books, how many weeks has he been buying them? Use long division to divide.

$$\begin{array}{r} 52 \\ 4)\overline{208} \\ -20\downarrow \\ \hline 08 \\ -8 \\ \hline 0 \end{array}$$

Dion has been buying papers for 52 weeks.

6. The Underwood family drove 2,005 miles in 9 days. How many miles did the Underwoods drive each day if each day's mileage was the same? How many more miles did they drive on the last day? Use short division to divide.

$$\begin{array}{r} 222 \text{ r7} \\ 9)\overline{2005} \\ {}^{2}{}^{2} \end{array}$$

The Underwood family drove 222 miles each day, except for the last day, when they drove 7 more miles.

Page 51

Mid-Test Chapters 1–3

Read carefully and solve. Show your work under each question.

A local school is selling tickets for its basketball games. The chart below shows the number of tickets sold for the first 4 home games.

Game	Number of Tickets Sold
1	978
2	8,652
3	13,478
4	4,799

1. How many total tickets were sold for the first 4 home games? Use the partition method to add.
   Thousands – 0 + 8,000 + 13,000 + 4,000 = 25,000
   Hundreds – 900 + 600 + 400 + 700 = 2,600
   Tens – 70 + 50 + 70 + 90 = 280
   Ones – 8 + 2 + 8 + 9 = 27
   25,000 + 2,600 + 280 + 27 = 27,907 tickets sold

2. Write the answer in expanded form and number name form.

   20,000 + 7,000 + 900 + 1

   twenty-seven thousand nine hundred seven

3. Out of the total number of tickets sold, only 11,956 people actually attended the games. How many people bought tickets but did not go to the games? Solve using a number line.

   $$\begin{array}{c} 6 \quad 50 \quad 900 \quad 1,000 \quad 10,000 \\ \overset{\frown}{15,951} \qquad\qquad\qquad 27,907 \end{array}$$

4. Round the answer to the nearest ten thousand: 20,000

112

Answer Key

Page 52

NAME

Mid-Test Chapters 1–3

Read the problem carefully and solve. Show your work under each question.

A sports team gave away 8,952 t-shirts at a recent home game. There were 14,560 fans at the game. At the next home game, the team gave away water bottles to 7,821 people. There were 15,322 fans at that game.

5. At the game where free t-shirts were given away, how many fans did not receive a free t-shirt? Use a number line to show your work.

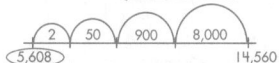

5,608 fans did not receive a shirt.

6. Out of the fans who did not get a t-shirt, 1,966 of them complained. How many did not complain? Draw a model to show your work.

3,642 fans did not complain.

7. Round the answer to the nearest hundred: __3,600__

8. Compare the number of T-shirts and water bottles given away. Use <, > or = to show which one was greater.

$$8,952 > 7,821$$

Spectrum Critical Thinking for Math
Grade 4
52

Chapters 1–3
Mid-Test

Page 53

NAME

Mid-Test Chapters 1–3

Read the problem carefully and solve. Show your work under each question.

Mr. Foster's Art Shop is ordering art supplies. Mr. Foster orders 36 boxes of paintbrushes. Each box holds 42 paintbrushes. Drawing pencils come in boxes of 213, and Mr. Foster orders 27 boxes. He also orders 8 boxes of colored pencils, and 19 colored pencils come in each box.

9. How many paintbrushes does Mr. Foster order? Use the traditional method to show your work.

$$\begin{array}{r} 36 \\ \times\ 42 \\ \hline 72 \\ +\ 1440 \\ \hline 1,512 \end{array} \text{ paintbrushes}$$

10. Write your answer in number name form:

__one thousand five hundred twelve__

11. Mr. Foster plans to have a sale on drawing pencils. How many drawing pencils does he order in all? Use the grid method to show your work.

He orders 5,751 pencils.

12. Round your answer to the nearest thousand: __6,000__

Spectrum Critical Thinking for Math
Grade 4
53

Chapters 1–3
Mid-Test

Page 54

NAME

Mid-Test Chapters 1–3

Read the problem carefully and solve. Show your work under each question.

Anton works at a paper warehouse. He ships 2 orders by truck. Anton wants to split each order equally among trucks. The first order contains 932 boxes of drawing paper. The second order contains 1,460 boxes of cardstock.

13. There are 8 trucks available to ship the order of drawing paper. How many boxes will Anton put on each truck? Solve using the partial quotients method.

$$\begin{array}{r} 116\ r4 \\ 8)\overline{932} \\ -800\ |\ 100 \\ \hline 132 \\ -80\ |\ 10 \\ \hline 52 \\ -48\ |\ 6 \\ \hline 4 \end{array}$$

Anton will put 116 boxes on each truck.

14. There are only 2 trucks left to deliver the cardstock. How many boxes will Anton put on each truck? Solve using long division.

$$\begin{array}{r} 730 \\ 2)\overline{1460} \\ -14\downarrow \\ \hline 06 \\ -6 \\ \hline 0 \end{array}$$

Anton will put 730 boxes on each truck.

15. The second truck is scheduled to make 5 delivery stops. How many boxes of cardstock will each stop receive if the boxes are split equally? Solve using short division.

$$\begin{array}{r} 146 \\ 5)\overline{7^{2}3^{3}0} \end{array}$$

Each stop will recieve 146 boxes.

Spectrum Critical Thinking for Math
Grade 4
54

Chapters 1–3
Mid-Test

Page 55

NAME

Check What You Know

Fractions and Decimals

1. $\frac{1}{4} + \underline{\quad} = \frac{2}{4}$

   $\frac{1}{4}$

2. Write an equivalent fraction for $\frac{2}{4}$.

   $\frac{4}{8}$ Possible answer: $\frac{2}{4} \times 2$ / $\times 2$

3. $\underline{\quad} - \frac{1}{9} = \frac{7}{9}$

   $\frac{8}{9}$

4. Write an equivalent fraction for $\frac{7}{9}$.

   $\frac{14}{18}$ Possible answer: $\frac{7}{9} \times 2$ / $\times 2$

5. Draw a picture to show the answers for #1 and #3. Then, write >, < or = to compare the fractions.

 <

Answer the questions. Show your work.

6. Westberg Bookstore received $\frac{2}{6}$ of its book order. The next day, it received $\frac{1}{6}$ of its book order. How much of the book order does the bookstore have?

$$\frac{2}{6} + \frac{1}{6} = \frac{3}{6}$$

The bookstore has $\frac{3}{6}$ of its order.

7. How much more of the book order does the bookstore have left to receive?

$$\frac{6}{6} - \frac{3}{6} = \frac{3}{6}$$

The bookstore is missing $\frac{3}{6}$ of its order.

Spectrum Critical Thinking for Math
Grade 4
55

Chapter 4
Check What You Know

Answer Key

Page 56

NAME _____

CHAPTER 4 PRETEST

Check What You Know

Fractions and Decimals

Add. Show your work.

8. $6\frac{4}{11}$
$+1\frac{3}{11}$

$$6\frac{4}{11}$$
$$+1\frac{3}{11}$$
$$\overline{\ 7\frac{7}{11}}$$

9. $8\frac{11}{12}$
$-1\frac{7}{12}$

$$8\frac{11}{12}$$
$$-1\frac{7}{12}$$
$$\overline{\ 7\frac{4}{12}=7\frac{1}{3}}$$

10. Amber is making 4 necklaces. Each necklace needs $\frac{6}{8}$ yard of string. How much string does Amber need for all 4 necklaces? Write the addition equation and the multiplication equation for each fraction. Then, solve. Write your answer in simplest form.

$$\frac{6}{8}+\frac{6}{8}+\frac{6}{8}+\frac{6}{8}=\frac{24}{8}=3$$
$$4\times\frac{6}{8}=\frac{24}{8}=3$$

11. Emily's plant grew $\frac{2}{10}$ of a centimeter. Justin's plant grew $\frac{40}{100}$ of a centimeter. How many centimeters did the plants grow in all? How can this be shown in a model? How can this be written as a decimal?

$$\frac{2}{10}=\frac{20}{100}$$
$$+\frac{40}{100}=\frac{40}{100}$$
$$\overline{\ \frac{60}{100}}$$

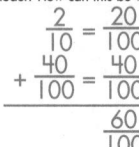

0.60

Spectrum Critical Thinking for Math
Grade 4
56

Chapter 4
Check What You Know

Page 57

NAME _____

Lesson 4.1 Equivalent Fractions

Follow the directions and answer the questions.

Multiply the numerator and the denominator by 6 to find an equivalent fraction.

$\frac{1}{3}=$ _____

$$\frac{1}{3}\times\frac{6}{6}=\frac{6}{18}$$

Divide the numerator and the denominator by 5 to find an equivalent fraction.

$\frac{10}{15}=$ _____

$$\frac{10}{15}\div\frac{5}{5}=\frac{2}{3}$$

Use multiplication to find an equivalent fraction.

$\frac{2}{4}=\dfrac{8}{\boxed{\ }}$

$$\frac{2}{4}\times\frac{4}{4}=\frac{8}{16}$$

Use division to find an equivalent fraction.

$\frac{15}{25}=\dfrac{3}{\boxed{\ }}$

$$\frac{15}{25}\div\frac{5}{5}=\frac{3}{5}$$

Jimmy has 24 diamonds. If $\frac{2}{8}$ of the diamonds are yellow, how many yellow diamonds does Jimmy have?

$$\frac{2}{8}\times\frac{3}{3}=\frac{6}{24}\qquad\text{6 of the diamonds are yellow.}$$

Spectrum Critical Thinking for Math
Grade 4
57

Lesson 4.1
Equivalent Fractions

Page 58

NAME _____

Lesson 4.2 Comparing Fractions

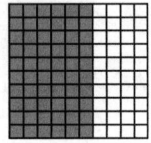

$\frac{2}{5}>\frac{1}{5}$

$\frac{2}{5}$ is greater than $\frac{1}{5}$.

$\frac{1}{3}<\frac{1}{2}$

$\frac{1}{3}$ is less than $\frac{1}{2}$.

$\frac{1}{4}=\frac{2}{8}$

$\frac{1}{4}$ is equal to $\frac{2}{8}$.

Draw a picture for each fraction. Then, write >, <, or = to compare the fractions.

$\frac{1}{5}\bigcirc\frac{2}{10}$

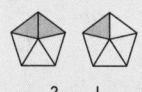 =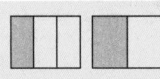

$\frac{3}{4}\bigcirc\frac{1}{2}$

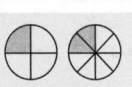

India and Hunter are making banners to carry in the town parade. India has finished $\frac{2}{8}$ of her banner, and Hunter has finished $\frac{1}{4}$ of his banner. Draw a picture for each fraction. Then, write >, <, or = to compare the fractions.

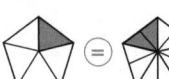 =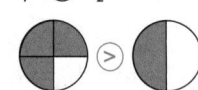

Hunter   India

Spectrum Critical Thinking for Math
Grade 4
58

Lesson 4.2
Comparing Fractions

Page 59

NAME _____

Lesson 4.2 Comparing Fractions

To compare fractions without pictures, the denominators must be the same. When you have unlike denominators, find the **least common multiple (LCM)** and rename the fractions.

$\frac{1}{7}\bigcirc\frac{2}{3}$

$\frac{1\times3}{7\times3}=\frac{3}{21}$

$\frac{2\times7}{3\times7}=\frac{14}{21}$

$\frac{3}{21}<\frac{14}{21}$

In the example, the denominators are 3 and 7, so find the LCM of 3 and 7.
Multiples of 3: 3, 6, 9, 12, 15, 18, ㉑, 24
Multiples of 7: 7, 14, ㉑, 28
The least common multiple of 3 and 7 is 21. To change each fraction so it has the same denominator, multiply both the numerator and denominator by the same number. Look at the numerator to determine the larger fraction.

For each fraction pair, write equivalent fractions with a common denominator. Then, compare the fractions.

$\frac{4}{8}\bigcirc\frac{2}{10}$

$\frac{4}{8}\times\frac{5}{5}=\frac{20}{40}\quad\frac{20}{40}>\frac{8}{40}$

$\frac{2}{10}\times\frac{4}{4}=\frac{8}{40}$

$\frac{3}{12}\bigcirc\frac{1}{3}$

$\frac{3}{12}=\frac{3}{12}\quad\frac{3}{12}<\frac{4}{12}$

$\frac{1}{3}\times\frac{4}{4}=\frac{4}{12}$

Morgan says that $\frac{2}{4}$ is the same as $\frac{8}{16}$, but Pilar says it is the same as $\frac{1}{2}$. Who is correct? Why?

$\frac{2}{4}\times\frac{4}{4}=\frac{8}{16}$

$\frac{8}{16}=\frac{8}{16}$

$\frac{1}{2}\times\frac{2}{2}=\frac{2}{4}$

$\frac{2}{4}=\frac{2}{4}$

They are both correct because $\frac{2}{4},\frac{8}{16}$, and $\frac{1}{2}$ are all equivalent.

Spectrum Critical Thinking for Math
Grade 4
59

Lesson 4.2
Comparing Fractions